P9-BIP-576

Higher Ground

A look at additional beliefs of Seventh-day Adventists

Morris L. Venden

Pacific Press Publishing Association
Boise, Idaho
Montemorelos, Nuevo Leon, Mexico
Oshawa, Ontario, Canada

4277

Copyright © 1984 by
Pacific Press Publishing Association
Printed in United States of America

Library of Congress Cataloging in Publication Data

Venden, Morris L.
  Higher ground.

  1. Seventh-Day Adventists—Doctrines. I. Title.
BX6154.V433   1984   230'.673   84-7792
ISBN 0-8163-0562-5
84 85 86 87 88 89 • 6 5 4 3 2 1

Introduction

In volume 1 of this series, *Common Ground*, we examined beliefs that Seventh-day Adventists hold in common with the rest of the evangelical Christian world. These include the divinity of Christ, the sinful nature of man, salvation by faith in Jesus Christ, heaven, the second coming of Christ.

In the second volume, *Uncommon Ground,* we looked at six major pillars of the Seventh-day Adventist faith that differ from beliefs held by the rest of the Christian world and give us our distinct mission and message. We saw that these are contained in the messages of the three angels of Revelation 14 and include the sanctuary and pre-advent judgment, the Sabbath, the law of God, the faith of Jesus, and the condition of mankind in death.

In this final volume we look at additional doctrines, some of which are shared and others that are more distinctive. In the first chapter we study the manner of Christ's coming, followed by a look at baptism, then the Communion service or Lord's Supper, stewardship, ethics or church standards, and spiritual gifts, closing with an invitation to decision.

No study of truth is ever complete. We can never sit back and say, "That's it. Now I have all truth." The invitation to *Higher Ground* will go forth as long as time lasts—and then throughout eternity we will still hear the voice of Jesus inviting us to come up higher.

This is what makes the central theme of these volumes so important. As we come into personal, daily, ongoing communion with Jesus Christ we are led continually to *Higher Ground*. In the end, no set of doctrines, no matter how theologically correct, will save the soul. Only as we come into personal fellowship with Christ, accept of His justifying grace, and walk day by day in relationship with Him will we be saved. And the uplifting of Jesus—in doctrines and beliefs, yes; but more than that—the uplifting of Jesus in our hearts and lives as well, is the only way to *Higher Ground*.

Contents

When Jesus Comes Again

My father used to tell the story of a man who decided to build a chimney. Of course, he needed brick and mortar. So he gathered these and put down his first course of bricks. Then he put down some mortar. After that he put down some more bricks and some more mortar. And then, of course, he put on more bricks and then more mortar! This can go on forever! I've discovered in telling the story to my own boys and girls that I get more tired telling it than they do listening to it!

There are stories that appear to go on forever. To some people, the story of salvation is one of them. It seems as if it has no end. That may be why Peter said, in 2 Peter 3:9, that "the Lord is not slack concerning his promise, as some men count slackness." The story of the plan of redemption does have an end. It's what the second coming of Christ is all about. Revelation 10:6 tells about an angel who stands with one foot on the land and the other on the sea and says, There shall be "time no longer."

Do you ever get tired of time? Are you weary of being a slave to the clock? A day is coming when that will change. We will stand on the verge of eternity, looking down a never-ending corridor in which there will be no such thing as time or clock. There will be time no longer!

I want to identify today with the millions of people who

believe that the second coming of Christ is not a fable or a fantasy but is real. It used to be that Seventh-day Adventists were the only ones who talked very much about the second coming, but it is a common belief to many people now. Anyone who believes in the second coming of Christ, or the second advent of Christ, is an adventist. So Seventh-day Adventists have been joined by Baptist adventists and Catholic adventists, and Methodist adventists and Presbyterian adventists.

Some who have studied Christ's second coming in Scripture, take the position that one fifth of the Bible has some reference to the event. The first preacher of the second advent that we know of is still alive—his name is Enoch. He preached on the second coming of Christ over 5000 years ago, and some people think that he even preached on the third coming of Christ. His prophecies are recorded in Jude 14, where he says that the Lord will come with ten thousand of His saints. Some say this is the second coming—but others say it must be the third coming. At the time of Christ's second coming, He will be accompanied by angels. It is when He comes the third time, bringing the New Jerusalem down to the earth, that He will be accompanied by ten thousand of His saints, the redeemed from this world.

So Enoch, who walked so closely with God, was the first advent preacher per se. We can still read the recorded part of his sermon! Isn't it interesting that he's still alive!

The Scriptures teach that all the prophets spoke of the coming of Christ. Let's notice Acts 3:19-21. In the middle of the sermon they preached to the doubting leaders in Jerusalem, as Peter and John pleaded, verse 19: "Repent ye therefore, and be converted, that your sins may be blotted out, when the times of refreshing shall come from the presence of the Lord; and *he shall send Jesus Christ,* which before was preached unto you: whom the heaven must receive until the times of restitution of all things, which God hath spoken by the mouth of all his holy prophets since the world began.'' He shall send Jesus! Note that all the holy prophets spoke of Jesus' coming, as did Peter and John on this particular day.

Now of course, the chief Prophet, Jesus Himself, said it in the well-known words of John 14, "I will come again.'' But notice the significant phrase that follows: "That where I am, there ye may be also.'' It is a law with which we are quite familiar that two people who love each other want to be together. Although Jesus is with us through His Spirit now, He wants to be with us in a fuller sense and without any veil between. His words indicate the deep love and regard, the emotional involvement that Jesus has with every one of His followers, "that where I am, there ye may be also.''

Revelation quotes Jesus as saying, "Surely I come quickly.'' Quickly? It doesn't seem like it! But let's remember how small time is in comparison with eternity. One of these days, what we thought was oceans of time will look like only a tiny drop in a huge bucket. And what we thought to be a great trial and horrible experience will seem as nothing when we look back on it from heaven's vantage point.

So we have all the prophets and all the apostles and Jesus Himself speaking of Jesus' coming. Martin Luther talked of it, although he said it probably wouldn't take place for at least 300 years after his time, which showed his insight into Bible prophecy. Modern preachers and theologians talk of His coming.

Now I'd like to consider more specifically the manner of Christ's coming and why there is so much misunderstanding concerning it. If you go into any popular religious bookstore, you discover that there are books galore on the subject of Christ's coming. Evidently there are many, many "adventist'' writers today. But the common thread through most of these books is what has been known for years as the secret rapture.

How anyone who knows Scripture can believe in the secret rapture is hard to explain. It must have something to do with more than just lack of information or with people neglecting to read their Bibles. I think it must have to do with the enemy of God himself.

I remember seeing an evangelistic title on a handbill years ago: "The Secret Rapture Ruptured!" It was a spectacular title, and contained a good idea. Why? Because the enemy who is behind the idea of the secret rapture has tried to rupture the facts concerning Christ's coming, and it's time *his* ideas were ruptured! I think he had personal reasons for misleading people concerning the second advent.

Revelation 14 gives the messages of three angels. The first says, "Fear God, and give glory to him." Has it ever occurred to you how much glory belongs to the One who made everything? If I were to design a sports car that would captivate thousands, the greatest honor and glory that could come to me would be that I had made the whole thing. Now of course, someone could come along and say, "Look at that fender!" Or, "Look at that hood!" Or, "Look at the way the lines drop, back there toward the rear of the car!" But the greatest total tribute and honor and glory would be in the fact that I created the whole thing.

There was a being in the universe, as you well know, who was determined to have the glory and honor that belong to God. Isaiah 14 quotes him saying, "I will be like the most High." He yearned to be above God. He ignored the fact that he had been created by God. It must gall the devil to realize, in spite of his thirst for power, that he wouldn't even exist if Jesus had not made him.

No wonder it galls him to read in his Bible (and don't you think the devil has one?) Christ's prophecy in Matthew 24:30, 31: "Then shall appear the sign of the Son of man in heaven: and then shall all the tribes of the earth mourn, and they shall see the Son of man coming in the clouds of heaven with power and great glory. And he shall send his angels with a great sound of a trumpet, and they shall gather together his elect from the four winds, from one end of heaven to the other.''

And in the very next chapter he can read Matthew 25:31: ''When the Son of man shall come in his glory, and all the holy angels with him, then shall he sit upon the throne of his glory.'' Now for a glory hound, that's got to be too much to take! When the devil first read it, I think he began to chew his fingernails and pace back and forth. He said, ''We'll have to do something about this!''

The devil knows that he cannot imitate the power and glory of Jesus' coming. He has only one third of the angels. But the more he thinks about the glory involved in the second coming, the more he is determined to detract from it. He's gone into his workshop and counseled with his imps, and they've come up with ways and means to change the whole picture. This is the most likely explanation I can come up with for the origin of the secret rapture.

The Bible is very clear, Revelation 1:7, that when Jesus comes again every eye will see Him. It's clear in Matthew 24:27 that as the lightning comes out of the east and shines unto the west, so will the coming of the Son of man be. It's clear in 1 Thessalonians 4:16, 17 that when Jesus comes down the vaulted skies there will be the great sound of a trumpet and the voice of the archangel, and the dead in Christ will rise. Those who are alive and remain will be caught up with them to the clouds. It will be the most world-shaking, cataclysmic event ever to have taken place.

The Bible is also clear, in 2 Peter 3:10, that even though ''the *day* of the Lord will come as a thief in the night,'' the event itself will be accompanied with ''a great noise.'' The last half of the verse says, ''The heavens shall pass away with a great noise, and the elements shall melt with fervent heat, the earth also and the works that are therein shall be burned up." There's nothing quiet or secret about that!

There is no way for a person with his eyes open to come up with the idea of a secret rapture. This is why I believe the enemy is behind it. He is the one who invented the idea that Christ will sneak in and sneak out, because he doesn't like to think of all that glory and honor going to Jesus.

. I heard a preacher depict the second coming of Christ in its secret version. He had a mock newspaper that had been printed with special headlines. He pictured "John" waking up the morning after Jesus comes. His wife is gone. He thinks, "She must be over at the neighbor's." After a while, he phones the neighbor, only to find that his neighbor's wife is also missing. They wonder what has happened to their wives. What's the answer? Jesus came last night and sneaked them off to heaven!

He had other headlines in his "newspaper," about bodies missing from the local morgue. What had happened? Jesus had come in the night. Then there was a story about an airplane crash. Jesus had come and sneaked off with the pilot and co-pilot, and woe to the people still on board, though perhaps a few passengers had gotten to go with the pilot and co-pilot.

So the preacher went on down through this mock paper, explaining all the excitement and consternation when, without any holy angels in the sky, without the trumpet and the shout and the glory, Jesus sneaked in and sneaked out. How preposterous! Yet thousands of Bible-reading Christians accept it.

If you can excuse just a bit of sanctified speculation, could it be possible that in the devil's attempts to fake Christ's coming, he may have taken over somewhere in the space program? If you've read very much about flying saucers, you know that there are heavy spiritualistic overtones. Whether Satan has anything to do with them or not, we know that when the events that precede Christ's second coming reach their culmination, Satan's deceptions will have an almost overmastering impact, deceiving if possible the very elect. See Matthew 24:24.

In spite of all of this, the God of heaven, to whom belong the honor and the glory and the power, is going to finish what He started.

He is coming to take those who are ready to meet Him. What does it take to be ready? It takes something more than wanting to be free from a world of trouble. It takes something more than wanting to escape from famine and earthquakes and tornadoes. It takes something more than wanting to be delivered from your enemies. That is precisely why the Jewish people in the days of Christ turned Him down at His first advent, because they were more interested in deliverance from the Romans than in deliverance from sin. It takes more than being sick and tired of trouble and pain and heartache and tears to be ready to meet Jesus when He comes.

It takes a realization that there is a God who loves us, and it takes a response to that God of love.

I've heard young people say, "I don't need God." But the question doesn't cross their minds, "Does God need me?" If God wants me in heaven, I'd like to be there, wouldn't you? If Jesus wants me there, I want to be there with Him.

Does it mean anything to you that Jesus, who died for you, wants you there? He owns the cattle on a thousand hills. He owns the gold and silver. The earth is His. But a day is coming when God will look down and say, "They shall be mine too." "They shall be mine, saith the Lord of hosts, in that day when I make up my jewels; and I will spare them, as a man spareth his own son that serveth him." Malachi 3:17. God is not happy with just cattle on a thousand hills. He's not happy with just gold and silver. He wants people. He wants you and me to be His as well. Jesus has promised that we can be among that group of people who make up His jewels when He comes again.

We read in Hebrews 9:28, "Unto them that look for him shall he appear the second time without sin unto salvation."

I was a freshman at college, and homesick. My brother had already been there for 2 years and knew everybody. I didn't know anyone. I was lonely. The first few weeks were a real trial.

One Friday I could take it no longer. I stuck a pack of Greek vocabulary cards in my pocket, thinking I would memorize them on my way and started walking the three or four hundred miles home. You can learn a lot of Greek in that much time! Only I didn't learn any Greek, because I was looking for a ride.

I stood in the desert sun for an hour. Ten rides later, under the cover of darkness, I found myself walking down the street of our block. I was home! I sneaked up on the porch and looked through the window. My preacher father was sitting by the fireplace going over his sermon notes for the next day. My mother was reading. I went to the door and threw it open, jumped in and said something that I had been known to say around home for a long time whenever I came in, "Let's eat!"

My father almost swallowed his Adam's apple, he was so surprised. He jumped up and came and hugged me. It was all that I had expected. But Mother? Mother just sat there quietly. I went over to her and kissed her and said, "Aren't you surprised, Mom?"

"No."

"How come?"

"I knew you were coming."

What it is in mothers, I don't know. They must have something inside that the rest of us don't have. But she knew I was coming. And one of these days when Jesus comes again there will be a group of people who will not be surprised, because they will have known He was coming.

Instead of their saying, "Let's eat," Jesus will say, "Come and dine." He will take them to a tree and pick the fruit and give it to them—fruit of the tree of life. They will live forever! Fantastic!

What a glorious day, when Jesus comes again!

Baptized Into Christ

"We are buried with him by baptism into death: that like as Christ was raised up from the dead by the glory of the Father, even so we also should walk in newness of life. For if we have been planted together in the likeness of his death, we shall be also in the likeness of his resurrection: knowing this, that our old man is crucified with him, that the body of sin might be destroyed, that henceforth we should not serve sin." Romans 6:4-6.

Perhaps you have heard about the woman who was married to a nit-picking, perfectionist husband. It was misery. The longer she lived with him, the more she realized that it was impossible to please him. If the potatoes were just a little bit too brown, it was dark blue Monday. If the house wasn't exactly right, things got really heavy. His preoccupation with perfection was so unbearable that one night, as she lay awake thinking of her terrible situation, she began trying to think of a way out.

She had vowed she would live with him "till death do us part." He was lying quietly beside her, and she thought, "Maybe I could just—." But that could get her into worse trouble! Then she thought of killing herself. After all, either he had to go or she did!

She realized that the ideal situation would be for her to die, thereby releasing herself from this marriage, and then come back to life and be married to someone else. I know this sounds rather complicated, but the Bible says that we must die to the sins we are married to and revive and live a new life married to Jesus. Read about it in Romans 6 and 7.

If you want to kill yourself there are a number of ways to do it. You can climb to the top of a high building and jump off. You can drop from the Golden Gate Bridge. You may be rescued by the Coast Guard, but the odds favor your success. You can load a six-shooter and put it to your head and pull the trigger. You can take an overdose of some lethal drug. But there is one way you cannot kill yourself. It's the Bible way. You must be crucified, and you cannot crucify yourself. Paul said, "I am crucified with Christ: nevertheless I live." Galatians 2:20.

As you read in the first few verses of Romans 7 the analogy of the nit-picking husband, you realize that the law says *you've got to do this,* and *you've got to do that.* And there's no way you can satisfy the law—or escape from it—because you are married to it. Death is the only way out. If you die to the law, Paul says, you can rise to a new life and be married to another. Jesus has made it possible for us to die with Him, be buried with Him in baptism, and rise again to live a new life with Him. It's what the symbol of baptism is all about.

In the Old Testament there were a number of ceremonies. In the New Testament, there are only three: marriage, the Lord's Supper, and baptism. Marriage was God's idea from the beginning; the Lord's Supper had its roots in the Passover service at the time of the Exodus. Baptism, however, is new in the New Testament, introduced to Christians by John the Baptist, and endorsed by Jesus.

Some people call these three ceremonies sacraments. To many Christians, *sacrament* involves the idea that the ceremony itself causes something to happen. Christians who think of baptism as a sacrament feel that baptism actually changes them. But the Protestant belief is that in baptism we are simply acknowledging an experience that has already occurred. People who have felt that baptism would do something to them in terms of changing their lives and freeing them from sin have often been very disappointed.

Once when I was visiting with a woman about spiritual things, she said, "Don't talk to me about baptism. I have been baptized three times, and not one of them took." She thought baptism was some sort of vaccination that would inoculate her against sin and temptation and failure.

This is why Protestants choose to call baptism a ceremony or an ordinance. It is a symbol. There is also in baptism, for the one who is looking for it, a very definite realization of the presence of God and of the holy angels, for the Bible tells us that there is joy in heaven when a sinner repents.

Seventh-day Adventists believe that there is only one form of baptism. The Greek word from which *baptism* comes means immersion. The early church had no question about it. It wasn't until about a thousand years after the time of Christ that any other form of baptism was introduced. The reason for the change was simple convenience.

Nobody is going to argue with that! It is not convenient for us ministers to leave the platform and change our clothes and get into the baptismal pool. It isn't convenient for the custodian to clean the baptismal pool and fill it and warm the water to the right temperature. It's not convenient for the baptismal candidates to get ready, and then get their hair wet, and have to dry off and dress again. It takes time, it is inconvenient, and some think it is embarrassing.

But may I remind you that Jesus is revealed in this service even in the inconvenience. Convenience doesn't happen to be an important criterion for some things we do, and it never has been the criterion for what Jesus does, either. It wasn't convenient for Jesus to travel the long journey from heaven to earth. It wasn't convenient for Him to be born as a babe in Bethlehem. It wasn't convenient for Him to fight a hand-to-hand battle with the devil for thirty-three years. It wasn't convenient for Him to feel a crown of thorns pushed into His temples. It wasn't convenient for Him to have His hands nailed to the cross. It wasn't convenient for Him to be forsaken by His Father.

Jesus demonstrated in His concern for us that He wasn't particularly interested in convenience. For us, He did some things that were most inconvenient.

John the Baptist could probably have thought of a more convenient method for baptism than going down into the water of the Jordan River. He did not find it convenient to be beheaded alone in a dungeon. It wasn't convenient for the disciples to die martyrs' deaths. Death wasn't convenient for the thousands who witnessed during the long dark centuries of religious persecution; or for Huss and Jerome, who were burned at the stake. There has never been anything convenient about always following God's Word. Convenience is not the issue. And I'm thankful that Jesus was willing to be inconvenienced, that through His poverty we might be rich.

So we're not going to belabor the point of immersion. It's the only form of Bible baptism, and you can check it out for yourself. You don't have to look very far.

Now let's look at the prerequisites for baptism. There are three: First, a person must understand. In the great gospel commission, Jesus told His followers, "Go ye therefore, and teach all nations, baptizing them in the name of the Father, and of the Son, and of the Holy Ghost." Matthew 28:19, 20. Notice the order: teach first, then baptize. This rules out infant baptism. "Teaching them to observe all things whatsoever I have commanded you."

When a person decides to be baptized, he admits publicly that he has been taught by God and understands. I know one young person who was promised a new Honda if he would be baptized. It's a naïve parent who would use that sort of leverage instead of "teaching them to observe all things."

Read the second prerequisite in Mark 16:16: "He that believeth and is baptized shall be saved; but he that believeth not shall be damned." Don't miss this, for the sake of those who have never had opportunity to be baptized. "He that believeth and is baptized shall be saved." The text does not say that he that believeth not and is not baptized will be lost. Eternal destiny is not decided primarily by baptism, because there are exceptions to the rule. Eternal destiny is decided by faith and trust in the Lord Jesus.

The thief on the cross was an exception to the baptism rule. Some people hide behind the thief on the cross. A pastor was urging a church member to become involved in missionary work. The church member said, "The thief on the cross never did any missionary work."

The pastor said, "Well, what about giving from our own funds to help people in foreign lands?"

The church member answered, "The thief on the cross never gave any money, and he's going to be in the kingdom."

Finally the pastor said, "It seems to me that the difference between you and the thief on the cross is that he was a dying thief and you are a living one."

It's not safe to hide behind the thief on the cross. However, if a person found himself in the same circumstances as the thief and could not be baptized, then the exception would apply, obviously.

For most of us the verse holds true as it reads, "He that believeth and is baptized shall be saved." It's a promise. Is the baptized Christian required to follow up with a lifetime of unblemished performance and good behavior? "He that believeth and is baptized shall be saved." There it is.

Read another text on baptism, Acts 8:36-38. Here is an exception to another rule. In most cases, baptism is designed to be a public confession of faith in Jesus, but there are exceptions as we see in this story of the first recorded Christian hitchhiker, Philip, and the Ethiopian treasurer. As the Ethiopian crosses the desert in his chariot, Philip climbs aboard and preaches from the Scriptures which the Ethiopian is reading. "And as they went on their way, they came unto a certain water: and the eunuch said, See, here is water; what doth hinder me to be baptized?" I've always liked that. "Here is water. What's wrong with my being baptized?" A simple question, but a profound act followed. "Philip said, If thou believest with all thine heart, thou mayest. And he answered and said, I believe that Jesus Christ is the Son of God." Notice that the mode of baptism was immersion. "He commanded the chariot to stand still: and they went down both into the water, both Philip and the eunuch; and he baptized him."

The third prerequisite for baptism is found in the same book, Acts 2:38. It is the day of Pentecost. Peter is preaching. In the middle of his sermon the congregation interrupts him. Notice verse 37: "When they heard this, they were pricked in their heart, and said unto Peter and to the rest of the apostles, Men and brethren, what shall we do?" Talk about altar calls—these people made their own!

Peter responded, "Repent, and be baptized every one of you in the name of Jesus Christ for the remission of sins." Repent. That's the third prerequisite. (1) Be taught. (2) Trust in the Lord Jesus. (3) Repent.

The Bible is very clear that repentance is not something *we* do any more than we can crucify ourselves. Repentance is a gift God gives. Let me explain. If repentance is being sorry for our sins and turning away from them, there's only one way it can happen. We must be sorry for something more than that we have not complied with two tables of stone that stare us in the face. Repentance is more than being sorry to displease a nit-picking husband who is never happy with the way the furniture is arranged. Repentance includes more than being married to the wrong person and being sorry about it. Repentance includes being married to the right person and loving him and being sorry when we disappoint him or let him down. It's realizing that he still loves us; it's being heart-broken because we have brought disappointment to this person we love. Repentance demands personal acquaintance with the Lord Jesus Christ. When we know Him as our best Friend and disappoint Him and bring sorrow to His heart as Peter did on the night of the denial, it breaks our hearts too, because of love. Repentance is all about broken hearts, not just a broken law.

That's why Romans 2:4 says the goodness of God leads us to repentance. His kindness, His love, His patience and longsuffering, the way He has borne with us through all our lives, and the way He is still following us even when we're running away—when you sense this love you fall to your knees in sorrow for having let Him down.

Remember that repentance involves a real, live, feeling Person who knows how to hurt and who weeps when people don't believe. Jesus wept at the tomb of Lazarus, not because Lazarus was dead—that was no problem to the Lifegiver. He wept because of unbelief.

The apostle Paul was reminded of the three prerequisites just before he became the apostle Paul. He had seen the bright light on the road to Damascus. His eyes had been blinded, and his heart was softened. Finally God sent him Ananias, a devout layman, who said to him, Acts 22:16: "And now why tarriest thou? arise, and be baptized, and wash away thy sins, calling on the name of the Lord." Don't wait, Paul. Don't tarry. Get up and be baptized. Provision has been made for your sins to be washed away. That's good news!

If the Lord Jesus could come to you, right now, in person, and walk straight up to you and look you in the eye and say, "I'd like to trade. I'd like to give you all of my righteousness and take all of your sins," would you trade? That is precisely what He wants to do, right now. How can you lose? Why do you wait? If you have been tarrying, perhaps for a long time, don't tarry any longer. Arise and be baptized and wash away your sins.

An older woman invited me to study with her at her house. We studied the gospel for several weeks, and one day she said she wanted to be baptized. In the process of our discussions, I had discovered that in her earlier days she had been a very wild person, caring nothing for God or faith or religion or standards of morality. Jesus had finally caught up with her. She had many lines on her face. If you let Jesus catch up with you early, you'll save a lot of facial lines. On the day of her baptism, before we went into the baptismal pool, she said to me, "Will you do me a favor?"

"Sure," I said. "What is it?" I didn't know what I was getting myself into!

She said, "When you get me under the water, I want you to hold me down under and count to ten, *slow*."

I said, "I beg your pardon?"

She said, "I'm serious."

I said, "Are you sure you can make it?"

She said, "Yes. I want to make sure that my sins are all washed away."

She was toying with the idea of a sacrament, perhaps! But she was sincere about it. She liked the symbol.

So I did. I held her down and I counted to 10, slowly. She was overjoyed!

Once in a while people ask questions about second baptism. What is the rationale behind it? According to Acts 19, there is a Bible reason for being baptized a second time. It doesn't have to do directly with growth in the Christian life.

It has to do with some truth you didn't know about and that you have been trampling upon or neglecting. When the believers in Acts 19 heard truth that they had been unaware of, they were baptized a second time.

Our practice in the Adventist Church has been to baptize someone a second time if he was once a Christian but had turned his back on God and gone his own way, then wanted to return. When such people become convicted that they want to renew their public confession of Jesus Christ, they are rebaptized.

Once in a while someone says, "I was baptized when I was 10 or 11 just because all of my friends were. I didn't really know what it meant. Since that time, I have died, but no one has attended my funeral. I have been born again, and nobody has celebrated my birthday. I'd like to be baptized for real this time." We don't hesitate when a person is convicted and convinced over a period of time that he wants this.

Some people say it's embarrassing to be baptized, and to some people it is. They want to be baptized privately, and it would be all right, I suppose, under the same circumstances and with the same Spirit direction as we find in Philip's baptism of the Ethiopian. But John the Baptist and Jesus proved that baptism, as a rule, is a public confession of the Lord Jesus.

Embarrassing? In my mind's eye I see a little woman in a crowd. She has been troubled for years with a hemorrhage. She is timid and retiring and bashful. Jesus is passing by. She slips through the crowd and manages just to touch the hem of His garment. She's healed! Now, ordinarily, when a person is healed, he jumps and shouts and praises God, even down the center aisle of the temple, like the lame man. But not this woman. Her timidity is greater than her joy. She is joyful, but she is so bashful she begins to fade into the crowd.

Jesus says, "Who touched Me?"

She freezes to the spot, stiff with fear.

Jesus insists, "Who touched Me?" Why? Did He want to embarrass a woman who would be more comfortable fading into the wallpaper somewhere? No. He knew that it would be for her good, not just His or the crowd's, for her to admit publicly what had happened to her. So it is in public baptism. Matthew 10:32: "Whosoever therefore shall confess me before men, him will I confess also before my Father which is in heaven."

We can be thankful for the privilege we still have today of baptism, and of confessing publicly our commitment to the Lord Jesus Christ.

Communion With Jesus

A Seventh-day Adventist evangelist was asked why Adventists keep the seventh-day Sabbath instead of worshiping with the rest of the Christian world on the first day of the week. The evangelist replied, "We believe in honoring the Sabbath as a memorial of creation, because that's what the Bible says, and we want to follow what the Bible says."

The one who was confronting him said, "No one *really* follows all that the Bible says. It can't be done. Why, if you really believed and followed all that the Bible says, you'd have to wash one another's feet."

To which the Adventist evangelist replied, "We do!"

There are very few people in the Christian church today who believe in three thirds of the Lord's Supper. There are some who believe in two thirds, and there are some who believe in one third. If we were to divide the service known as the Communion service into its three parts, we would have the ordinance of foot-washing, the cup, and the bread. Some Christian churches take only the bread, and others take the bread and the cup. Only a few take all three parts.

Now, of course, different people call the Communion service by different names. One church calls it a sacrament. Others call it the ordinance of the Lord's house. Some call it the Communion service, and others refer to it as the Lord's Supper. Different labels, but the same basic service.

The Bible record of the foot-washing service is found in only one chapter, John 13. All four Gospel writers talk about the Lord's Supper. However, only John talks about all of the three parts. Let's read the pertinent verses, beginning with the first of John 13.

"Now before the feast of the passover, when Jesus knew that his hour was come that he should depart out of this world unto the Father, having loved his own which were in the world, he loved them unto the end. And supper being ended, the devil having now put into the heart of Judas Iscariot, Simon's son, to betray him; Jesus knowing that the Father had given all things into his hands, and that he was come from God, and went to God—" What an introduction! What a prelude to the rest of the story! But it's significant. Please notice especially the last part of that prelude. "Jesus knowing . . . that he was come from God, and went to God."

Jesus knew who He was. He knew that He was going to go back to His Father. He knew that He was God. He knew from whence He came, He knew that He was the Creator, He knew that He was the One who had spoken the worlds into existence. If anyone ever deserved glory and honor, it was Jesus. He knew all that. Then John tells what He did, beginning with verse 4.

"He riseth from supper, and laid aside his garments; and took a towel, and girded himself. After that he poureth water into a bason, and began to wash the disciples' feet, and to wipe them with the towel wherewith he was girded."

Do you see the contrast? What a solemn, subduing effect it has on the human heart! You can see a sample of the time when Jesus was in heaven and rose from His throne, laid aside His kingly garments, and girded Himself in the form of humanity, to come to earth to become the servant and Saviour of all mankind.

Then comes the story of Peter, which we will skip over

for now and go down to verse 12: "After he had washed their feet, and had taken his garments, and was set down again, he said unto them, Know ye what I have done to you? Ye call me Master and Lord: and ye say well; for so I am. If I then, your Lord and Master, have washed your feet—" Here is reason number one why we should wash feet: "Ye also ought to wash one another's feet." Now for reason number two: "For I have given you an example, that ye should do as I have done to you. Verily, verily, I say unto you, The servant is not greater than his lord; neither he that is sent greater than he that sent him." Here comes reason number three: "If ye know these things, happy are ye if ye do them."

So what are the three reasons for continuing the ordinance of foot-washing? Jesus says we ought to, He is our example, and we will be happy if we do it.

Are you happy to wash someone's feet? Are you really happy to get your feet washed during this ordinance? I suspect that there are people who find real meaning in the service, who find Jesus revealed in it. If they partake of this service one Sabbath and it happens that they visit another church the next Sabbath where the communion service is being held, they are overjoyed. But I have also met people who, if they have partaken of the service in one church and they come to another church the next Sabbath where the communion service is being held, they say, "We already did that for this quarter. We're not going to do it again!" They figure they've already put in their time!

Some deliberately absent themselves from the service each quarter because they find it distasteful and repulsive. As one woman said, "Why, washing someone's feet! That's what you do in a hospital! You don't do that in church." A student said to me, "I usually wash my feet myself!" Could it be that there is a message here—to let someone else do for you what you usually do for yourself?

One of my favorite questions when we're having this ordinance is to ask the person that I'm participating with, "Which do you find it harder to do, to wash someone else's feet, or to have yours washed?" The usual answer is that it is harder to have someone else wash your feet. Why? Is it embarrassing? Is it a private thing, that you don't really want to expose your feet that publicly? Or is there something deep down inside that resists being dependent upon someone else?

Is it possible that many of us pretend not to be humiliated or embarrassed during the service, though we really are? The give-away may be the mundane topics we so often talk about. One of the most interesting things is to watch a group of Adventist people washing feet. Embarrassed to tears, they're trying to act as if they aren't! This has led some of us to take this position: Maybe there's something good about being humbled; maybe, instead of trying to fight it and act as though it isn't happening, we ought to admit our humiliation and seek for the good that is involved in what is sometimes called the "ordinance of humility." It can be humbling to have someone wash your feet, and it can be humbling to wash someone else's.

With that in mind, let's go back to the section in our scripture about Peter, John 13:6 and onward. "Then cometh he to Simon Peter: and Peter saith unto him, Lord, dost thou wash my feet? Jesus answered and said unto him, What I do thou knowest not now; but thou shalt know hereafter. Peter saith unto him, Thou shalt never wash my feet." So Peter found it hard to have his feet washed. But why? Peter knew that Christ was the Son of God, and he figured Christ had no business doing this sort of menial task. He was feeling guilty already for not having volunteered himself.

In those days, it was the custom before a group proceeded too far in an evening's activities for a servant to wash the dusty feet of the guests; and if no servant was available, then someone volunteered. Of course, you can't expect a volunteer from a group of disciples who have been arguing about who will be greatest. I mean, if you're planning to sit on the right hand or the left hand of the coming king, you don't go around washing people's feet.

Peter was humiliated at the thought of Jesus' washing his feet. But Jesus said, "If I wash thee not, thou hast no part with me."

Verse 9: "Simon Peter saith unto him, Lord, not my feet only, but also my hands and my head." We've always smiled and liked Peter for that! "Jesus saith to him, He that is washed needeth not save to wash his feet, but is clean every whit." Peter had already had his hands and head washed at baptism. I suppose that's why we sometimes say that foot-washing is a miniature baptism. It's suggested, even though it's not actually stated.

Then Jesus said a strange thing: "Ye are clean, but not all. For he knew who should betray him; therefore said he, Ye are not all clean." Who was the exception? Judas. So that meant the rest of them were clean. But they had just been arguing about who was to be the greatest. Yet Jesus said, "Ye are clean." How can you get that together? Notice this comment from the classic book on the life of Christ, *The Desire of Ages*, page 646: "Peter and his brethren had been washed in the great fountain opened for sin and uncleanness. Christ acknowledged them as His. But temptation had led them into evil, and they still needed His cleansing grace. When Jesus girded Himself with a towel to wash the dust from their feet, He desired by that very act to wash the alienation, jealousy, and pride from their hearts. This was of far more consequence than the washing of their dusty feet. With the spirit they then had, not one of them was prepared for communion with Christ. Until brought into a state of humility and love, they were not prepared to partake of the paschal supper or to share in the memorial service which Christ was about to institute. Their hearts must be cleansed. Pride and self-seeking create dissension and hatred, but all this Jesus washed away in washing their feet. A change of feeling was brought about. Looking upon them, Jesus could say, 'Ye are clean.' Now there was union of heart, love for one another. They had become humble and teachable. Except Judas, each was ready to concede to another the highest place. Now with subdued and grateful hearts they could receive Christ's words.''

So we have the example of Peter and the lesson in Jesus' words, that if we want to have a part with Him we must get involved in this service. If He does not wash us, we have no part with Him.

In the early church it was customary for the ordinance of foot-washing to be a part of the Lord's Supper, but gradually it faded away. It's inconvenient, so it was easy to leave it out. But Seventh-day Adventists still believe in it and practice it, because it's what Scripture teaches.

There are different formats for the Lord's Supper in our different churches. Sometimes we sing, and sometimes we meditate. You know good and well that the service doesn't mean much to you when you're spending the time talking about weather and neighbors and the latest news. Some of us have discovered that even when we talk from the platform about the importance of speaking about spiritual things during the foot-washing service, or simply being silent, it makes no difference! We go out immediately to the service, and the talk goes on just the same. Another thing that some have noticed is that as soon as we've taken the grape juice, while many still have the cup to their lips, a great *clickety-clackety-click* rises from the rows of seats as people who have gulped the wine stick their glasses into the little holders as fast as they can. That bothers some of us. Perhaps we're being ultrasensitive. But are we really trying to rush through the service and get it over with, or are we thinking carefully and solemnly about what we're doing? Is this a duty, or is it a real blessing?

The Spirit of God is especially near during the Communion service. The word *communion* attached to the service is not a bad label. The entire Christian experience is all about communion with God. The Communion service is a time when communion is going on, ideally, a two-way communication. God is particularly eager to communicate with us at this time.

The Communion service originated in the upper room, with Jesus and His disciples. They were gathered to celebrate the Passover, which was a celebration of deliverance from Egypt. So a key word for the Communion service is deliverance.

We are familiar with what Egypt stands for. It has to do with all that is dark and sinful and against God. We're familiar with the miraculous deliverance of God's people from Egyptian bondage. We're familiar with the night the Israelites killed the lambs and sprinkled the blood on the doorposts. One of the main purposes of the Communion service is to sprinkle Christ's blood on the doorposts of our hearts.

I suppose the people back there could have asked a lot of questions. "What good will it do to sprinkle blood on doorposts?" But God had said to do it, and those who believed Him did it. People today wonder what good washing feet accomplishes. But Jesus said to do it, and those who love and follow Him find meaning in it and in gathering together at the Lord's table.

Finally, I'd like to remind you of three deliverances we celebrate in the Communion service. First, deliverance from the guilt of sin. God has promised, "If we confess our sins, he is faithful and just to forgive us our sins." 1 John 1:9. The forgiveness was provided at the cross, through the Lamb of God.

The second deliverance we celebrate is deliverance from the power of sin. "If we walk in the light, as he is in the light, we have fellowship one with another, and the blood of Jesus Christ his Son cleanseth us from all sin." 1 John 1:7. Usually we think of the blood of Christ as bringing forgiveness, but notice that the blood delivers *us* from sin as well.

Would you be free from your burden of sin?
There's power in the blood, power in the blood;
Would you o'er evil a victory win?
There's wonderful power in the blood.

Third, we celebrate a deliverance that hasn't happened yet, the deliverance from a world of sin when Jesus comes again. Do you ever grow tired of sin and sickness and pain and fear and death and tombstones and battered babies and suffering millions? The day will come when Jesus will return. This is the Christian hope. Jesus referred to it when He celebrated that first Communion service. He said, "As often as ye eat this bread, and drink this cup, ye do show the Lord's death till he come." 1 Corinthians 11:26. Till He come. He's coming again!

So going way back to Egypt, when believers sprinkled blood on doorposts and were delivered before morning, we can still remember and celebrate deliverance today, the deliverance that comes through communion with Jesus as we accept His grace and power.

World's Greatest Robbery

A minister of a Congregational church told me, "I think it's fabulous the way the Seventh-day Adventist people give their tithes. I've been trying to get my church to do the same."

If he could have gotten ten people to pay 10 percent, he could have kept that as his salary and would have had the average income of those ten people. If he could have gotten the ten in his congregation who had the highest incomes to pay 10 percent, he would have had the average income of the ten most wealthy in his congregation. Wouldn't that have been nice?

One of the things that makes it comfortable for ministers of the Adventist Church to talk about money is the fact that the Seventh-day Adventist minister does not receive the funds that the people in the local church give in tithes and offerings. All the tithe that comes to the local church is sent to the local conference, a certain percentage goes on to the North American Division, and a certain percentage to the world field. The funds are then distributed according to the economic scale of the country in which a minister serves.

For example, in the United States, one minister may have a district with two churches—one with 40 members and the other with 14. I had one that size once. That minister receives almost the same salary and benefits as the pastor of the largest church in the nation.

This does away with the idea that if you have a larger congregation, you can pull for more funds. It completely relaxes the ministers in the church to approach the question of tithes and offerings on the basis of Bible truth alone, with no personal ax to grind.

Another thing that makes it comfortable for a Seventh-day Adventist minister to talk about money is the fact that ministers pay tithe too. So we can study together to find what the Bible teaches about money and giving.

Let's begin by looking at an Old Testament verse, Psalm 24:1. Here we discover who owns everything. "The earth is the Lord's, and the fulness thereof; the world, and they that dwell therein." Now consider Haggai 2:8: "The silver is mine, and the gold is mine, saith the Lord of hosts." Now turn to Psalm 50:10-12. God is talking again. "Every beast of the forest is mine, and the cattle upon a thousand hills. I know all the fowls of the mountains: and the wild beasts of the field are mine. If I were hungry, I would not tell thee: for the world is mine, and the fulness thereof." God sounds rather possessive here, doesn't He? But He is the One who created everything, so He has a right to say, "It's Mine." Are you willing to give Him that right?

Some people say, "This proves that God is selfish. He's possessive. He's self-centered." This has always been one of the devil's charges against God. But the cross did away with that argument.

Notice something else, from Deuteronomy 8:18. Notice where even the wealth that we consider our own comes from. "Thou shalt remember the Lord thy God: for it is he that giveth thee power to get wealth, that he may establish his covenant which he sware unto thy fathers, as it is this day." Is it possible to be legitimately wealthy? Can you think of any Bible examples of people who were? What about Abraham or Job or Jacob? It isn't wrong to be wealthy. God gives power to get wealth. The important thing is to remember that it is God who has that power. He is the One who is responsible.

Whatever the amount of our "wealth," the Bible teaches that a portion is to be returned to God. Leviticus 27:30 says that all the tithe belongs to the Lord, whether the tithe of the land, or of the seed of the land, or of the fruit of the tree. The tithe, or 10 percent, is to be set aside for a special purpose. Numbers 18:21: "I have given the children of Levi all the tenth in Israel for an inheritance, for their service which they serve, even the service of the tabernacle of the congregation." So the Old Testament principle was that those who ministered in the temple were supported by the tithe.

Some think that tithing is an Old Testament teaching and that Jesus downed the idea. We've been reading primarily Old Testament references so far, so let's take a look at the New Testament now. In Matthew 23:23 Jesus seems to diminish the importance of tithing when He says to the scribes and Pharisees, "Ye pay tithe of mint and anise and cummin, and have omitted the weightier matters of the law, judgment, mercy, and faith." But the verse doesn't end there. Notice the rest of it: "These ought ye to have done, and not to leave the other undone." So Jesus wasn't throwing tithing out but was using it as a basis of comparison to show the importance of other truths.

Another New Testament reference to tithing is found in 1 Corinthians 9:13, 14: "Do ye not know that they which minister about holy things live of the things of the temple? and they which wait at the altar are partakers with the altar? Even so hath the Lord ordained that they which preach the gospel should live of the gospel."

Then in verse 15 Paul goes on to say that he hadn't always taken advantage of this himself. He sometimes made tents for a living. But he still upheld the truth that ministers of the gospel should be supported by the gospel, even though he hadn't insisted on it personally. So here we find that the purpose of the tithe, even in New Testament times, was to support the ministry.

Well, where should we put our tithe? Some feel they should be able to do with it as they please, giving it wherever they see a need. I met a man who believed he could give 10 percent of his talents instead of 10 percent of his money. He was good on the violin. He worked out a system whereby he would play a special number in Sabbath School and count that as his tithe for the month. But let's notice what the Bible teaching is on this point.

Malachi 3:8-11: "Will a man rob God? Yet ye have robbed me. But ye say, Wherein have we robbed thee? In tithes and offerings. Ye are cursed with a curse: for ye have robbed me, even this whole nation. *Bring ye all the tithes into the storehouse,* that there may be meat in mine house, and prove me now herewith, saith the Lord of hosts, if I will not open you the windows of heaven, and pour you out a blessing, that there shall not be room enough to receive it. And I will rebuke the devourer for your sakes, and he shall not destroy the fruits of your ground; neither shall your vine cast her fruit before the time in the field, saith the Lord of hosts." Italics supplied.

So where is the tithe supposed to go? Do you know where the storehouse is? Is it a cigar box underneath the bed springs? Let's let the Bible interpret itself. Nehemiah 13:12: "Then brought all Judah the tithe of the corn and the new wine and the oil unto the treasuries." Treasuries. If you have a margin in your Bible, you can look at the reference there. It probably says, "or storehouses." Then there is the text in Malachi 3:10 which we just read. Now look at Nehemiah 10:38: "The priest the son of Aaron shall be with the Levites, when the Levites take tithes: and the Levites shall bring up the tithe of the tithes unto the house of our God, to the chambers, into the treasure house." Notice the idea running through these verses of a common treasury at the church.

Sometimes people worry about misappropriation of funds and whether or not they should bring their funds to the storehouse if they don't agree with the decisions of whoever has been placed in charge of the treasury. One of the greatest misappropriations of funds is found in Exodus 32. The Israelites had brought great wealth out of Egypt because on the last night they had "spoiled the Egyptians." Then, at Sinai, Aaron had them bring the gold to him to make a golden calf. You'll have to admit this was a gross misappropriation. They ended up drinking it. See Exodus 32:20.

God showed at Sinai that He knew what was going on and that He was still in charge. He didn't tell the people to stop bringing their gold to the treasury simply because the funds had been misused in this particular incident.

A few years ago I was pastor of a church that had a problem with the local church school. It was always in trouble financially. One of the local businessmen had decided to pay all his tithe into the school budget to try to keep the school open, instead of sending it to the church treasury. But the school was still in deep trouble.

Some of the school-board members discovered that he was using his tithe this way and decided that God could not bless the school program if this sort of thing were allowed to continue. They made it clear to him that they no longer wanted his money if it came from tithe.

He was a little hurt at first, but he was later impressed when the church school, without his tithe, quickly went into the black and stayed in the black.

Another man in the same church had been sending his tithe to a certain mission station he knew about. He was also sponsoring a student through medical school, and he was supporting a needy family. He had several worthy projects that he kept going with his tithe. The church began to study this question of bringing the tithe into the storehouse, or church treasury, from whence it is to be dispersed by the church organization.

This man went through quite a struggle. He didn't know what to do. But one night he told me that he had finally made his decision to turn in 10 percent to the storehouse—but that he was going to pay an additional 10 percent to keep supporting the mission station, the medical student, and that needy family. That month his business profits jumped phenomenally and stayed up after that. He joined the rest of the people who have tried it, but who have never succeeded in outgiving God. Have you tried? You cannot outgive God!

I take the position that God has given us a carte blanche in Malachi 3, and although there is a much greater blessing in giving for the right motives, God has even made provision for His promise to be fulfilled when we give for bad motives! I've seen it happen. I've had it happen.

This is the only place I know of where God has said, "Test me." Some have decided to pay tithe for business purposes, and have discovered that God's promise is sure even in those circumstances, where noble motives like love and gratitude are left out. When you make a similar discovery, I expect you will want to improve your motives. Try it and see if I'm right!

Statistics show that probably only 50 to 60 percent of Seventh-day Adventists are faithful in tithing. This varies from place to place, but church members who do not pay tithe are simply showing (1) a lack of faith, (2) ignorance, or (3) poor judgment. Tithing is the smart thing to do! It is a proven fact that nine dollars with God's blessing goes much farther than ten dollars without His blessing. If you've tried it, you know it is true. Even eight dollars with God's blessing goes farther than ten dollars without.

So far we have talked about tithe. I must include tithes *and offerings*. God has been robbed in tithes *and* offerings, according to Malachi 3. Some who are very faithful tithe payers give very small offerings. They forget that when they have paid God 10 percent, they have only been honest. They have not yet been generous. Freewill offerings are in addition to the 10 percent.

One of Jesus' heaviest teachings on the subject of giving was in His relationship to the little widow in Mark 12:41-44. Notice what happened. "Jesus sat over against the treasury, and beheld how the people cast money into the treasury: and many that were rich cast in much. And there came a certain poor widow, and she threw in two mites, which make a farthing." The gift was very small; our economy changes so rapidly that the equivalent is different all the time. But it was about the smallest gift possible in their currency.

Jesus "called unto him his disciples, and saith unto them, Verily I say unto you, That this poor widow hath cast more in, than all they which have cast into the treasury: for all they did cast in of their abundance; but she of her want did cast in all that she had, even all her living."

What is the lesson of this story? That Heaven places value upon the gift in an entirely different way than we do. Jesus said this little woman gave more than the rest, because God measures our giving, not by the amount we give, but rather by what we have left after we have given.

If someone puts in $10,000 and has $10,000 left, he has given less than someone who puts in two pennies and has nothing left.

I've heard people say, "I gave all the money I had." But what about your possessions? If you have put in your last two pennies of cash but still have a house in the city and another in the country and a mountain cabin and a boat on a lake and a Winnebago in the garage, you have given very little. Jesus told the rich young ruler to sell what he had and give. He was to dispose of some of his investments. Possessions can sometimes hinder giving. It is still true that

"where your treasure is, there will your heart be also."
Matthew 6:21. If our treasure is invested largely in things
that perish with the using, they can be a major stumbling
block to spiritual life.

As we noticed earlier, this does not mean that it is wrong
to be wealthy. Nicodemus was wealthy, and his wealth
blessed the early church. Other righteous men have used
their wealth to sustain God's cause. Wealth becomes a
problem when it is used to excuse a failure to sacrifice when
God calls for means. It is legitimate to have a base from
which to make more money, so long as a person is willing at
any time God says to sell everything, or so long as he is willing and eager to use his increase for the purpose God sees
best.

When we refuse to give, refuse to bring our tithes and offerings to the Lord, we are the ones who lose. When we see
the love God has for us, we will be willing to give all we
have and are to Him. We love because He first loved us, and
we give because of His gift to us. Second Corinthians 8:9:
"Ye know the grace of our Lord Jesus Christ, that, though
he was rich, yet for your sakes he became poor, that ye
through his poverty might be rich." We can be thankful for
His gift of Himself and the blessing that He offers each day
for those who return to Him a portion of what He has so
freely given.

Jesus Revealed by Your Appearance

Do you like to claim Bible promises? Here's one for you. Isaiah 59:2: "Your iniquities have separated between you and your God, and your sins have hid his face from you, that he will not hear." Or, if you prefer, here's Psalm 66:18: "If I regard iniquity in my heart, the Lord will not hear me." Are you interested in claiming those promises? Or do you find yourself wondering what this kind of text means?

We can know to begin with that they do not mean God won't hear sinners who are trying to come to Him, because if they did, we would be in the same fix as the man whose horn didn't work. He went to the garage to get it fixed and saw a sign on the door, Honk for Service. An impasse! So these texts cannot refer to the sinner who wants to come to Jesus for forgiveness and power. Logic and reason forbid it!

Could it be that these texts speak to the person who has been convicted of sin and is holding on to the sin stubbornly by keeping away from relationship with God? Even though we can always come to Christ for forgiveness and pardon and power to overcome, we insult Him when we refuse His forgiveness and power and come instead asking for special blessings. God has all kinds of blessings to pour on people, but if He gave them to those who are living apart from Him, it would only establish them in their selfishness.

Is it possible to be a professed Christian and still live apart from Christ, and thus be full of pride and selfishness? What is the worst sin? What was Lucifer's sin? Pride! He said, "I will exalt my throne above the stars of God. . . . I will ascend above the heights of the clouds; I will be like the most High." Isaiah 14:13, 14.

Which brings us to the question of the way we dress and appear! You ask, "How does pride bring that in?" Well, how could it *not* bring it in? Let me ask you some questions.

Is there anything wrong with washing your face? Is there anything wrong with combing your hair? How about wearing a watchband? Is it OK to wear a necktie? Should a Christian's clothes be in style? Should Christians try to look nice? Are scarves or pins acceptable? What about lace, ribbons, and buttons? Is it wrong to dye your hair or wear a wig? Is it wrong to wear make-up? If a wristwatch is all right, what about a pendant watch? Is there any difference between wearing a colored scarf and a small silver necklace? Is all jewelry forbidden? What about a wedding ring?

Where does pride of appearance begin and end? Should we allow for differences of opinion on the subject, according to background and culture?

If there is a gray area in religion, it certainly includes dress and adornment! In many instances, there is no chapter and verse to tell us where to draw the line.

Let's notice first the Bible principles on the subject. In Revelation 12 God uses a woman to represent a true, pure church. Verse 1: "There appeared a great wonder in heaven; a woman clothed with the sun, and the moon under her feet, and upon her head a crown of twelve stars." What kind of clothing is indicated here? Simple things.

Now let's go to Revelation 17:4, 5, which speaks of another woman who represents a fallen, impure church. She is actually called a whore in the King James version. Notice how she is dressed. "The woman was arrayed in purple and scarlet colour, and decked with gold and precious stones

and pearls, having a golden cup in her hand full of abomina-
tions and filthiness of her fornication: and upon her fore-
head was a name written, MYSTERY, BABYLON THE
GREAT, THE MOTHER OF HARLOTS AND ABOMI-
NATIONS OF THE EARTH." It is easy to see in Revelation the contrast between God's symbols for a pure woman
and a corrupt woman.

We must try to understand these symbols in light of the
rest of Scripture and not try to make them stand on all fours.
I suppose there might be people who don't believe in wearing anything at all who would find comfort in Revelation 12,
in the clothed-with-the-sun type of thing. That interpreta-
tion would be contrary to God's Word, however, because
God has something else to say about nakedness, doesn't
He? So we know that He is talking about simplicity and natural appearance as contrasted with the description in Revelation 17.

Let's go on to Isaiah 3, one of the main Old Testament
records of how God feels about certain types of jewelry and
ornaments. I'm not going to give you a phrase-by-phrase ex-
position of Isaiah 3, for some things listed there are not as
familiar to us as they were to the people of that time. But the
chapter mentions (in verses 16-24) ornaments, chains,
bracelets, earrings, jewels, and pins. Most of these we are
familiar with. God has a real burden concerning them. They
are symptoms of an inner lack. So often what a person lacks
on the inside he tries to make up for on the outside! But
when a person has the qualities of grace on the inside, he
doesn't have to make up for them on the outside.

Just how appropriate dress should be defined, and exactly where the lines should be drawn can be complex
sometimes. It is tragic that so often people who are beautiful
on the outside rely on externals and are quite empty on the
inside. On the other hand, some of the plainer people I have
met, on the outside, were beautiful inside. After a while I

began to think they were beautiful on the outside too. Have you ever had that experience? It happens when someone is full of the fruits of the Spirit. Even in a secular, worldly sense, you can see the same thing. But it is particularly demonstrated in the life of a Christian.

Let's read two major texts from the New Testament. Find 1 Timothy 2. The setting in verse 4 is that God wants everyone to be saved. In verse 8, Paul says, "I will therefore that men pray everywhere, lifting up holy hands, without wrath and doubting. In like manner also," verse 9, "that women adorn themselves in modest apparel, with shamefacedness and sobriety; not with broided hair, or gold, or pearls, or costly array." What is the reason for this rule, according to the context? It evidently has something to do with the church's witness, that all may be saved.

The other text is 1 Peter 3:3, 4, where Peter talks especially to Christian wives, "whose adorning," he says, "let it not be that outward adorning of plaiting the hair, and of wearing of gold, or of putting on of apparel; but let it be the hidden man of the heart, in that which is not corruptible, even the ornament of a meek and quiet spirit, which is in the sight of God of great price."

We have often confined the subject of dress to women. But if there was ever a time when it ought to include all of us, it's today. Some men stand for hours in front of a mirror blowing and brushing their hair, so let's make these principles apply to everyone. Christians should not become preoccupied with external concerns that draw attention to themselves. We should instead focus our attention on the inner graces.

One of the main reasons for this moderation is our witness to others, so that people will see past the exterior to the inner graces of the heart and character. The question of dress and how we appear does not have as its major intent the cause or means of our salvation, but is simply an evidence of the experience of the person who has accepted salvation.

I remember a little town in southern California where I would go to give Bible studies every Tuesday the first year I was in the ministry. Coming to that meeting was a young couple who were neighbors of a church member. The young wife looked like Revelation 17. In fact, she looked like Revelation 17 twice! Even by the standards of the world, she was overdone. She had half a dozen chokers and earrings down to the shoulders—the whole business!

However, she and her husband were very much interested in the good news of salvation. They wanted to stay after the Tuesday night meetings and study more. Before we were finished, we were meeting twice a week, because they were so eager to learn.

A strange thing began to happen. The more we studied about Jesus and salvation, the more Revelation 17 began to disappear. It was almost a drama to watch. She went from 6 chokers to 5 to 4 to 3 to 2. Her earrings shrank from the shoulders to half-way to just small ornaments. I don't know where she stashed them all, but she had a different length for each week's Bible study! The make-up faded from purple to red to pink, right down to natural. One day I came and there were no ornaments. They were both chewing on pieces of board and eating carrots.

I said, "What's going on?"

"We're trying to quit smoking." Now mind you, we hadn't said anything about jewelry or adornments or smoking.

But about this time I got suspicious that some nit-picking church member had been beating them over the head with church standards. So I began to quiz them. "Why are you trying to quit smoking?"

"Well, we just feel like it."

"Someone been talking to you about it?"

"No."

"You sure?"

"Yes."

Then I finally made bold to bring up the rest of it, including Revelation 17. But nobody had talked. They had read nothing on it. As Jesus had come in, these things had dropped off. It was not that we never talked of these things, for we did study about them later. They were interested in all of God's Word. But the changes began first.

The same principle applies within your own home. If you make a religious issue out of something in the realm of externals with your young people, before they have had a personal relationship with the Lord Jesus, it may make them unhappy enough with God and religion to postpone their personal relationship with the Lord Jesus for some time.

If I, as a parent, choose to make an issue over externals before my child knows a personal relationship with Jesus, I would be wise to make that issue purely on the basis of my own wants and preferences and leave God clear out of the picture. I don't want to use God as a lever and have Him blamed for spoiling my young people's fun. Does this mean you never look at these issues? No. But you do your best to keep the peripherals and externals from coming first, and turning young people away from God before they have come to know Him as a friendly God. The starting place must always be with the heart and fellowship with God.

I have discovered as I move from one pastorate to another that Adventists in one part of the world are pretty much like those in the rest of the world. There are two types almost everywhere—those who know God and those who don't. And, at least within our Adventist subculture, those who know God think pretty much alike and look pretty much the same on the outside. But the people who don't know God are like chameleons; they turn the color of whatever their surroundings may be. If they happen to be in a conservative environment, they look conservative. If they move to a more liberal area, it takes them only a few weeks to look like the liberals.

Behavioral scientists tell us that it's healthy to want to be accepted by the group, that it's a natural human tendency to want to be part of the crowd. But I can tell you that you will be soon crippled if your decisions on moral issues are based on what the herd does.

I was driving along a turnpike in Ohio soon after the white line had been painted. The paint was still wet and there were No Passing signs all along the way. I got tired of driving slowly, and when the man in front of me pulled across the newly painted line to pass, I did too! So did the officer who was driving behind me!

He pulled us both over, and after he had finished talking to the other man, he asked me, "Did you see the signs?"

"Yes."

"Why did you do it then?"

I said, "Because the man ahead of me did." What a stupid answer! I should never have used it. I have always remembered his reply.

He said, "If he had jumped off the Brooklyn Bridge, would you have jumped too?"

Often, the problem with fashion and style and outward adornment is not so much in the things themselves but in our preoccupation with them. When our focus and attention is on what the crowd is doing and wearing instead of on the Lord Jesus Christ and our personal relationship with Him, our spiritual life suffers.

Is it possible for Jesus to be revealed through our appearance? Let's read about Jesus in Isaiah 53: "Who hath believed our report? and to whom is the arm of the Lord revealed? For he shall grow up before him as a tender plant, and as a root out of a dry ground: he hath no form nor comeliness; and when we shall see him, there is no beauty that we should desire him. He is despised and rejected of men; a man of sorrows, and acquainted with grief: and we hid as it were our faces from him; he was despised, and we esteemed him not.''

We understand that Jesus was not the most outstanding person in outward appearance, but He was still the most beautiful person who ever walked the earth. Why? Because of what came out from within.

Regardless of changing mores and differing cultures, I would like to have more of the inner adornment, wouldn't you?

If you want gold, buy gold tried in the fire, which is faith and love. If you want pearls, look for the Pearl of great price, which is Jesus. Accept from Him the inner beauty that can shine out to others arround you and draw them to His love. 4277

The Battle for Your Mind

I have a recipe for angel-food cake that you may like to try. First, get out the angel-food cake pan. Then put in some garbage—nice, fresh garbage. Next, find the old frying pan you forgot to clean after last summer's camping trip and scoop up some scrapings off the bottom and put them in. Find a bone that some dog has been chewing in the front yard and put it in. Last, open a can of raspberries and pour in some milk and let it do what it does! Stir these ingredients together, let them rise for half a day and put the mix into the oven for half an hour. I can assure you on the basis of all the laws of nutrition that you will not get angel-food cake! For it is a painful reality that what goes into the oven is what comes out. Sometimes what comes out is even worse!

We are not what we think we are, but what we *think*, we are. Isaac Watts described that truth in verse:

Were I so tall to reach the pole,
   Or grasp the ocean with my span,
I must be measured by my soul:
   The mind's the standard of the man.

With that setting, let's notice an interesting text found in Luke 11:21, 22: "When a strong man armed keepeth his palace, his goods are in peace: but when a stronger than he shall come upon him, and overcome him, he taketh from him all his armour wherein he trusted, and divideth his spoils."

There is a similar verse in Mark 3:27: "No man can enter into a strong man's house, and spoil his goods, except he will first bind the strong man; and then he will spoil his house."

Who is the strong man? Within the human frame, the mind is the strong man of the human being. The "stronger man" who comes trying to destroy us is going to have to bind the strong man first. This must refer to Satan. But, thank God, there is One even stronger yet, the Lord Jesus Christ.

The battle in this great conflict is the battle for the mind. The devil knows all the tricks and has saved some of his best for last.

I don't know how long it will take you to guess that we are referring to health and how it relates to the other doctrines of the church.

The Bible makes it clear that it is the mind that counts. First Samuel 16:7: "Man looketh on the outward appearance, but the Lord looketh on the heart." God has always looked at the heart; and when we speak of the heart, we refer to the mind.

In the beginning, before we come into personal relationship with the Lord Jesus, we have what is called in Scripture a carnal mind (see Romans 8:7), or a sinful mind. God has made provision through the gospel to renew our minds. Let's read Romans 12:1, 2: "I beseech you therefore, brethren, by the mercies of God, that ye present your bodies a living sacrifice, holy, acceptable unto God, which is your reasonable service." Other versions say, "for this is your spiritual worship." If people do not keep their bodies holy, they are unfitted to be spiritual worshipers. Going on with verse 2: "Be not conformed to this world: but be ye transformed by the renewing of your mind, that ye may prove what is that good, and acceptable, and perfect, will of God."

There's a very close cousin to the text in Ephesians 4:23,

which you may wish to look up for yourself in your further study of the subject. It talks again about the renewing of the mind. The renewal takes place at conversion.

Seventh-day Adventists believe in the harmonious development of the physical, mental, and spiritual powers. They have long emphasized this. Some people think that the way you take care of your body has nothing to do with religion. But we believe it has a lot to do with religion and believe the Bible is very clear on this point.

People often say, "Seventh-day Adventists? Oh, they are the people who believe in keeping Saturday for Sunday and who don't eat meat." Although diet is important, more is involved in healthful living and in the battle for the mind than simply diet. We can remember the words of Jesus, "These ought ye to have done, and not to leave the other undone." Matthew 23:23.

Let's notice in John 14:21-23 that Jesus promised His disciples and His followers of every age that He would come and dwell with them. "He that hath my commandments, and keepeth them, he it is that loveth me: and he that loveth me shall be loved of my Father, and I will love him, and will manifest myself to him. . . . And we will come unto him, and make our abode with him." How does God manifest Himself to us? One way is by sending the sunshine and rain. But He does that for everyone, even for the skeptic and the agnostic and the atheist. So He must be talking about doing more than that for faithful Christians who love and obey Him. He must plan to communicate with them more directly. I like the way it's said in the book *Education*, page 209: "The brain nerves that connect with the whole system are the medium through which heaven communicates with man, and affects the inmost life. Whatever hinders the circulation of the electric current in the nervous system, thus weakening the vital powers and lessening mental susceptibility, makes it more difficult to arouse the moral nature."

The most important part of the human brain is the cerebrum. Here is the higher center of the mind where communion with God, sensitivity to the Holy Spirit, and conscience reside. The first part of the brain that is damaged by the use of stimulants is this higher center. A person may still be a successful businessman or mathematician; he may be able to function in daily life, even if his spiritual center is knocked out. The devil, being a master physiologist, knows all about the fine line between what it takes to keep a person operating on a secular basis and at the same time keep him dead spiritually. It is possible to "blow your mind" by mistreating the higher centers of the brain. Some young people, with reckless abandon, have done this, forgetting that the mind is their most precious possession. They have discovered that a time comes when even the powers of reason and judgment no longer operate.

This is the way the enemy has worked to bind the strong man of the human system. The brain resides in the body. Because of this, there is a close relationship between the mind and the body, so that whatever affects the body affects the mind. The higher centers of the mind, where God communicates with man, are often first to be affected when the body is abused.

So what does insufficient sleep do in terms of affecting communion with God? What does a lack of exercise do in terms of affecting communion with God? What does sitting up to watch television's late-late show do to your communion with God? What do drugs and alcohol do to your communion with God? The strong man gets bound, and the devil spoils our goods. It's just that simple. The devil has done a masterful job of spoiling goods. We see spoiled goods on every hand, ruined hearts and livers and lungs and lives. Many of us have experienced the spoiling of our goods at one time or another, and there are people everywhere who are victims of it.

Why do we consider this such an important subject? Well, the Bible uses some strong language concerning it. Notice two texts. First, 1 Corinthians 6:19, 20: "What?" That's an interesting way to begin a verse, isn't it? "What? know ye not that your body is the temple of the Holy Ghost which is in you, which ye have of God, and ye are not your own? For ye are bought with a price: therefore glorify God in your body, and in your spirit, which are God's." Now the other one, 1 Corinthians 3:16, 17: "Know ye not that ye are the temple of God, and that the Spirit of God dwelleth in you? If any man defile the temple of God, him shall God destroy; for the temple of God is holy, which temple ye are." The wording reminds us of Daniel and his three companions, who would not defile themselves with the delicacies from the king's table. What you eat and drink, whatever you do, is very significant in terms of spiritual life.

When it comes to health and healing, there are eight natural remedies, which work as preventive medicine as well. Preventive medicine sounds at first as if it were some kind of program to prevent people from taking their medicine! Instead, it's a method to prevent people from needing to take medicine.

I met a doctor in northern California who appeared to be of retirement age. I asked him, "Are you retired?"

He said, "Oh, no! I'm just getting started!"

"What do you mean?"

"Why," he said, "I've been practicing medicine for thirty or forty years and ripping people off! I've just found out how to practice medicine, and I'm so excited I can hardly wait to get to the office every day."

As we talked more about it, I discovered that he was into preventive medicine. He was so excited about it that I finally had to walk away in order to meet my next appointment. He wouldn't let me go, because he was so excited about what he was doing!

There are many ways of practicing the healing arts. But God's remedies are the simple agencies of nature: pure air, sunlight, abstemiousness, rest, exercise, proper diet, the use of water, and trust in divine power. These are the true remedies.

What is a remedy? A remedy is a solution to a problem that has already developed. So these are remedies, but also preventives. They are both the means to recovery and the means to keep from getting sick in the first place.

A pastor is often contacted by people who have problems with their health. Some of us have gotten up enough courage to hang out our shingle without a license. We prescribe these eight natural remedies, and I can testify to some real success in practicing medicine this way.

Someone gave me this poem:

> The best six doctors anywhere,
> And no one can deny it,
> Are sunshine, water, rest, and air,
> Exercise and diet.
>
> These six will gladly be your friends,
> If only you are willing.
> Your ills they'll mend, your cares they'll tend,
> And charge you not a shilling.

Written by the British, obviously! It takes in six of the eight natural remedies, sunshine, water, rest, air, exercise, and diet. To bring in the others, I have made up a couple of lines!

> The cure for bad lasciviousness
> Is *trust* and good *abstemiousness!*

Why don't you check yourself out? How are you doing on these eight? Usually when someone is in trouble health-wise, he has been falling short on two or three or even more of these eight simple remedies. Examine your own life sometime.

I don't make any apologies for practicing medicine this way. The eight remedies not only have physical benefits, there is a spiritual counterpart for each one as well.

Sunshine. Jesus is the Sun of Righteousness.

Water. Through Jesus we are invited to partake of the water of life.

Rest. Matthew 11:28. Come unto me and I will give you rest. Hebrews 4 speaks of the Sabbath rest.

Air. What is the breath of the soul? Prayer. It is one of the major ingredients for a healthy spiritual life.

Exercise. What's the spiritual counterpart? Christian service, witness, and outreach.

Proper diet. Jesus, the Bread of Life, revealed in His Word.

Abstemiousness. What's another word for that? Moderation or temperance or self-control. Self-control is one of the fruits of the Spirit. See Galatians 5:23. It is not something you get by working on it. Some of the most miserable people in the world are the ones who are trying to generate self-control. It's like trying to generate love. It is impossible to love by trying to love—love is the result of something else.

And *trust* in divine power, which is already a spiritual quality.

Let's return to the subject of health in a physical sense. Seventh-day Adventist take a strong stand against alcoholic drinks, narcotics, and stimulants. Other denominations once shared this emphasis but have gradually become more liberal.

We believe, according to the Bible and according to statistics, that strong drink is a real enemy. Someone has written, "As a remover, alcohol has no equal. Alcohol will remove all grass stains from summer clothes. It will remove summer clothes, too, also spring and winter clothes, not only from the man who drinks it, but also from his wife and children. It will remove household furniture from the house and food from the pantry. It will remove the smile from the face of the wife and happiness from the home. Yes, as a remover, alcohol has no equal.''

Several years ago someone figured out a way to succeed in the drinking business. His recipe is a bit humorous, but it speaks truth.

''Build a bar in your own home and be the only customer. This way you do not have to buy a license. Give your wife six dollars to buy the first quart of liquor, remembering that there are at least sixteen snorts in a quart. Buy your drinks from no one but your wife, and pay at the regular rate you would at a local bar. By the time the first quart is gone, she will have six dollars to put in the bank and six dollars to start up business again. If you live for ten years and continue to buy from her, then die with snakes in your boots, she will have enough money to bury you, educate your children, marry a decent man, and forget she ever knew you.''

That's the lighter side of it, but it makes sense. Experts who study the statistics on highway accidents and crime warn us that we have not been told the whole story. We spend billions of dollars for research on sickness and disease and health problems, but we spend far more every year on the results of strong drink, stimulants, narcotics, and drugs—and spend almost nothing trying to stop their use. Seventh-day Adventists believe this has a lot to do with religion, not just because the church says so, but because Satan, the strong man of the world, has discovered the strong man of the human soul and knows where to hurt him.

As long as we are dealing with specifics, let's look at diet. Why do Adventists in general believe in a vegetarian diet? Is it because we are nit-picking legalists, trying to spoil good meals? No! Some of us are vegetarians because we were brought up that way; we wouldn't know what to do with a piece of meat if someone put it on our plate. But there is a deeper spiritual reason involved too, besides health and freedom from disease. That is, meat eating resulted from sin. If there hadn't been sin, there would be no death, and if there were no death, there would be no meat eating. So when sin is no more and death is no more, there will be no more meat eating. People who are taken from this world to the next will not experience a sudden change in their appetites. Our characters will not be changed when Jesus comes. So it makes sense to begin now to get used to the way we are going to live then, doesn't it? More is involved in the battle for your mind than food and drink. Television must be included. Stimulants can be found in the medicine cabinet, true, but also in the family room! The battle for the mind is a lifelong conflict. The premise in the on-going Christian life is that what gets our attention, gets us.

We do not have the power within ourselves to protect ourselves from the enemy. Our strong man is forced to recognize that there is someone stronger than he. And the stronger one is intent on keeping the goods he has spoiled. But there's a promise in Isaiah 49:24, 25: "Shall the prey be taken from the mighty, or the lawful captive delivered? But thus saith the Lord, Even the captives of the mighty shall be taken away, and the prey of the terrible shall be delivered: for I will contend with him that contendeth with thee, and I will save thy children."

We are captives of Satan, but God has promised to deliver us. Isn't that good news? When Jesus was here, He won the battle against one who is stronger than we are, and He made it possible for people who were hopeless captives to be set free by the renewing of their minds. He has power today to renew our minds and set us free from the power of the strong man who has kept us in bondage.

Black, White, or Gray

How do you decide what is right and wrong? Some things are black and some are white, as everyone will agree. But many things appear to be neither black nor white but gray. You can't find chapter and verse for them. All you have to go by is what someone has told you, or your own feelings and convictions on the subject. How do you decide?

One person says, "Stay in the middle of the road." But where is that? Would the middle of the road be right for Laodicea? If there is such a church as lukewarm Laodicea, surely the middle of the road would be the worst place for it!

Another frequently suggested method is to ask, "What would Jesus do?" Whole books have been written on that. But can there be different ideas of what Jesus would do? If you were reared in a conservative home, you might be unable to picture Jesus bowling or shooting pool. If you came from a more liberal background, it might be perfectly acceptable in your mind for Jesus, and for you too, to bowl and to shoot pool. I've heard church members argue about church standards at length. How are we to decide for sure?

Most of us know of black areas where we really don't have any trouble deciding. We could define black as anything expressly forbidden in Scripture. We could define white as anything we are specifically invited to do in God's Word. But what about the gray? The devil has done his best to introduce a lot of gray. It's nice stuff for his purposes. He can get people from white to black through the gray zone. The devil doesn't find it nearly so easy to take people from white straight to black, so he goes through the gray.

Church standards contain many gray areas. Where do we draw the line when choosing what music to listen to? Where do we find specific information on what entertainment is acceptable for the Christian? What books should we read, what television programs should we watch? For many of these things, there is no chapter and verse that tells exactly what to choose. We can find general principles in Scripture, such as 1 John 2:15-17, "Love not the world, neither the things that are in the world. If any man love the world, the love of the Father is not in him. For all that is in the world, the lust of the flesh, and the lust of the eyes, and the pride of life, is not of the Father, but is of the world. And the world passeth away, and the lust thereof: but he that doeth the will of God abideth for ever." The general principles help, but when it comes to making the specific application, there are many differing ideas of what is acceptable.

There are two major ways to approach this dilemma. The first is the logical approach, which many of us have used almost exclusively. I propose that the logical approach is not sufficient. In the Garden of Eden, Satan said, "Go ahead and eat, because if you do, you will be as gods, knowing good and evil." But can we trust logic? Is any of us wise enough to distinguish exactly what is right and what is wrong when there is no chapter and verse for it? Logic can help us decide, but something more is needed.

However, let's examine what we *can* use in the area of logic. First, examine the motive behind the action. Proverbs 4:23: "Keep thy heart with all diligence; for out of it are the issues of life." And in 1 Samuel 16:7 the Lord said to Samuel, "Man looketh on the outward appearance, but the Lord looketh on the heart." It is important for all to become familiar with the tenor of their conduct from day to day, and with the *motives* which prompt their actions. Not every action is judged by the external appearance. Many are judged by the motives that prompted them.

The second logical approach to a gray-area question is to avoid the appearance of evil. Read 1 Thessalonians 5:22: "Abstain from all appearance of evil." The principle of avoiding the appearance of evil can give a logical basis for helping to decide.

A third logical principle is influence. There are three chapters you can read which give real help on this one—Romans 14, 1 Corinthians 8 and 10. Read each for yourself; we'll look at excerpts here. Romans 14:7: "None of us liveth to himself, and no man dieth to himself." Verse 10: "Why dost thou judge thy brother? or why dost thou set at nought thy brother?" Verse 12: "Every one of us shall give account of himself to God." Verse 13: "Let us not therefore judge one another any more: but judge this rather, that no man put a stumblingblock or an occasion to fall in his brother's way." Verse 16: "Let not then your good be evil spoken of." Verse 21: "It is good neither to eat flesh, nor to drink wine, nor any thing whereby thy brother stumbleth, or is offended, or is made weak."

Look at 1 Corinthians 8:9: "Take heed lest by any means this liberty of yours become a stumblingblock to them that are weak." Then notice the principle in verse 10, "If any man see thee which hast knowledge sit at meat in the idol's temple, shall not the conscience of him which is weak be emboldened to eat those things which are offered to idols; and through thy knowledge shall the weak brother perish, for whom Christ died? But when ye sin so against the brethren, and wound their weak conscience, ye sin against Christ. Wherefore, if meat make my brother to offend, I will eat no flesh while the world standeth, lest I make my brother to offend."

In those days food was at times dedicated to idols and then later sold in the marketplace. Paul was speaking here to the question whether food that had been dedicated to idols was acceptable for Christians to eat. Some felt it was; others felt it was wrong. Instead of giving a hard-and-fast rule, Paul said, in essence, that they were to eat the food if someone would be offended if they didn't, but they were not to eat it if someone would be offended if they did. At first glance it looks as if he's being wishy-washy. But let's look a little further, 1 Corinthians 10:23 and onward: "All things are lawful for me, but all things are not expedient: all things are lawful for me, but all things edify not. Let no man seek his own, but every man another's wealth [or good]. Whatsoever is sold in the shambles, that eat, asking no question for conscience sake." On to verse 28: "But if any man say unto you, This is offered in sacrifice unto idols, eat not for his sake that shewed it, and for conscience sake: for the earth is the Lord's, and the fulness thereof: conscience, I say, not thine own, but of the other: for why is my liberty judged of another man's conscience?" Verse 32: "Give none offence, neither to the Jews, nor to the Gentiles, nor to the church of God."

I don't know what you get from this, but two things appear to be opposites. One is, Don't judge someone else; don't stumble over what someone else is doing. The other is, Don't do anything to cause someone else to stumble. They sound paradoxical, don't they? Evidently Paul is trying to protect a person who is weak in faith, a newcomer perhaps, who has not had a chance to grow and mature; he realizes that it is possible to cause someone else to stumble.

It was my rare experience to drop down out of the sky one week to pastor a new parish. It was a thousand miles from where I had been before. No one there knew me, and I knew no one. My family was back home, getting ready to move, and I was overdue at the new church.

When I arrived, I took my suit to the cleaners in town and attended prayer meeting in other clothes the first night. I sat on the back row.

After the meeting, the elder who had led out came back and said, "Who are you, anyway?"

I said, "I'm your new pastor!"

He said, "I thought so."

Sabbath came. I had picked up the suit from the cleaners—which turned out to be the most expensive cleaners in town. They had put a silk hankie in the pocket. It was fake; it had cardboard on the bottom! But it looked nice, so I left it in and preached the first Sabbath in the new church.

After church someone invited me to dinner. I learned that everyone was talking about what a certain brother had said that day. He had passed it up and down the row where he sat. He had said, "Watch this new preacher. Watch him. He'll leave the message. He'll go into apostasy."

"Why?"

"He has a hankie in his pocket."

When I heard that, my first impression was to put in two hankies the next week, one of them red! Then I began to think. If I did that, I'd have problems too, wouldn't I? Obviously this brother had problems. I didn't think, and I still don't think, that it makes any difference to God whether I have a hankie in my pocket or not. Where do you draw the line in outward adornment? You could draw the line the other side of combing your hair in the morning, couldn't you? The more I thought about it, the more I was certain this man had a problem. I'm supposed to be his pastor, and I would like to help him with his problem, so that he will look at something besides hankies in preachers' pockets. I'm sure that he's never going to hear anything I say the whole time I'm here if I keep wearing the hankie. So I took it out, and I did not wear a hankie in my pocket anymore.

I faced reality. I didn't need it. It was not very utilitarian with cardboard on its lower half! And if there was a possibility that one brother was going to stumble, I could afford to go without it.

I'd like to end the story with some sort of success like his becoming a world religious leader or something. All I can say is that the channel remained open, we had many good visits and became good friends. Whatever impression was made upon him, only eternity will tell. But the issue of influence can be an important one.

One final clue, logically speaking, for making decisions for things we do not have chapter and verse for in the Bible is the question, Where will it lead? Proverbs 16:25: "There is a way that seemeth right unto a man, but the end thereof are the ways of death." Here is a premise vital to every question that's black, white, or gray. The devil never takes a person from black to white in one jump, as we have already mentioned. He takes him in little steps. Sometimes the only thing wrong with step number one is that it leads to step number two.

The mind of a man or woman does not come down in a moment from purity and holiness to depravity, corruption, and crime. It takes time to transform the human to the divine, or to degrade those formed in the image of God to the brutal and satanic. It takes time for a sinner to be transformed into the image of God, and it takes time to capture an innocent babe and drag him downhill to where he can commit horrible crimes. It takes time to go from babyhood to killing six million Jews. It doesn't happen in one big jump, but in little steps. It is the direction of those tiny steps that decides the direction of the life.

So if there's nothing morally wrong with step number one and I cannot decide on the basis of black and white or chapter and verse, but if I have found by experience, or if I have seen in the experience of others that it is a convenient way toward step number two or three, then it's worth my while to consider backing clear away from that first fateful step.

Television provides a handy illustration. We bought a TV once, to watch only the coronation of Queen Elizabeth and the men going to the moon and Walter Cronkite. Before long we began adding other programs. Isn't this the way it works? "Maybe this one would be all right," we say, then add another. And what about the kiddies? "Let's add one for the kiddies!" Soon the family circle turns into a semicircle.

Let's suppose you are the pastor of a church. One night you come home from prayer meeting and sit up to watch the late-late show—a murder mystery! It's all right, because it has a missionary in it! After it finishes, you get out the clippers and cut the plug off the end of the electric cord. The TV sits idle for several days.

But then Queen Elizabeth gets crowned again, and your wife cuts the insulation off the wires and pokes them into the socket. This little drama continues, until when you finally sell the TV it has a six-inch cord!

You smile because you are well aware of that syndrome. The pattern has been repeated in many homes, including perhaps your own. It shows that the enemy has saved some of his best tricks for last, and he uses the gray, the downward pattern of little-by-little, step-by-step. So we need to ask, Where will this lead? There is a way that seemeth right, but the end is the way of death.

Logic alone cannot provide a final answer in the gray areas, and so I'd like to go on to what I consider to be the only ultimate answer. God must provide insight into the hidden motives of our hearts.

Isaiah 30:21 says, "Thine ears shall hear a word behind thee, saying, This is the way, walk ye in it, when ye turn to the right hand, and when ye turn to the left." I will discern that voice only if my channel is open. You have to have an open channel to the voice of God, and you won't have it unless you have an ongoing relationship with Him. The person who all of a sudden decides he wants to find out what's wrong about a given thing but who doesn't have ongoing communion with God will find great difficulty getting God's signals straight. Jesus said in John 10:4, 5, "When he [the shepherd] putteth forth his own sheep, he goeth before them, and the sheep follow him: for they know his voice. And a stranger will they not follow, but will flee from him: for they know not the voice of strangers." If we are being guided by the Good Shepherd day by day, we will recognize His voice and not go astray.

In John 16:8, 13, Jesus said that the Holy Spirit would convict of sin and righteousness and that He would guide into all truth. But we must be open to His guidance. We have been promised in Philippians 2:13 that God will work in us "to will and to do of his good pleasure." *To will* means "to choose." If I surrender myself to God in a trusting relationship with Him, He will make the choices for me; and He will back up the choices He makes for me with the power of heaven. Paul explained this in Galatians 2:20: "I am crucified with Christ: nevertheless I live; yet not I, but Christ liveth in me: and the life which I now live in the flesh I live by the faith of the Son of God, who loved me, and gave himself for me."

When God lives in us, and is doing His thing in us, we can be certain that He wills to do the right thing, can't we? "Those who decide to do nothing in any line that will displease God, will know, after presenting their case before Him, just what course to pursue. And they will receive not only wisdom, but strength."—*The Desire of Ages,* p. 668.

So in order to understand without doubt concerning the gray areas for which you cannot find chapter and verse, you must have a personal, ongoing relationship with Jesus day by day. He has a way of flashing His signals to you, so you will know His will.

Some denominations today list what's acceptable and what's unacceptable, and sometimes we have fallen into that trap. We have a corner in the *Adventist Review,* our church paper, where people can write in and ask whether they should leave the potatoes in the oven on Sabbath! But should we stand around giving judgments concerning what's right or wrong when the Bible has not spoken specifically? Shouldn't we say, "Go to your knees!"

Often members phone the pastor to ask, "Will you tell me if this is right or wrong for me to do?"

All the pastor can say is, "To your knees, my friend, to your knees!" It's the only way to deal with the gray areas.

Isn't it a tragedy that so often we try to see how close we can get to the edge and still make it through. What a strange thing for professed followers of Christ to do!

The story is told about a stage-coach company in the East, years ago, who needed a new driver. They interviewed three men and asked each the same question, "Do you know that dangerous place along the mountain pass where the precipice goes straight down on one side and straight up on the other, and the road is so narrow?" All three drivers knew about it.

They asked the first driver, "How close can you come to the edge of the precipice and still take the stagecoach through?"

He said, "I can drive within a foot of the edge and still make it safely."

They asked the second driver, "How close can you come to the edge?" And he said, "I can drive within six inches of the edge and still get through safely."

When they asked the third man, he said, "I don't know how close I can go, but I'll tell you one thing. I'm going to stay as far away from the edge as I can." The third man got the job.

"Those who feel the constraining love of God, do not ask

how little may be given to meet the requirements of God; they do not ask for the lowest standard, but aim at perfect conformity to the will of their Redeemer. With earnest desire they yield all and manifest an interest proportionate to the value of the object which they seek. A profession of Christ without this deep love is mere talk, dry formality, and heavy drudgery.''—*Steps to Christ*, p. 45.

When you go to Gethsemane, you don't see a middle-of-the-road moderate trying to see how little He can get by with. The Man sweating drops of blood has not been trying to ride the middle of the road. When you look at Jesus, you see a Man who was totally dedicated to His mission. He was not trying to see how little He could do and still save the world—He went the limit. You see it in His followers. And you see it in the three Hebrew worthies who were not afraid of the fire. You see it in a man who was not afraid to open his window and pray three times a day, when, if he had had the New Testament, he would have had a good excuse for praying in the closet!

Down through the centuries, prophets and apostles and martyrs were not middle-of-the-road moderates. They manifested an interest in proportion to the value of the object they sought.

I'd like to propose that the answer to television or music or any of the other questions in the gray areas is found in the relationship with Jesus. When Jesus comes in, some of these things that we thought so big and important are crowded out, and we have no more problem. I like to know the answers that come from logic and reason as far as they go, for Jesus invited us to reason together. But I'm more interested in the answers that are signaled to us personally, from heaven.

Spiritual Gifts From God

Friends of ours were driving through Salt Lake City with some new converts to the Seventh-day Adventist Church. They toured the large temple and heard about the beliefs of the people there. Presently the new converts remarked, "We're sure glad the Seventh-day Adventist Church doesn't have any of this business of prophets."

Our friends went hot and cold, and everything got kind of black. They didn't know what to say, so they said nothing. Obviously the new converts had been rushed into the church too fast. Prophets have a lot to do with God's church. The gift of prophecy has had much to do with God's people in all ages. God has designed the gift to be in the church until the end of time. It you don't believe in the gift of prophecy, you don't believe in the Bible. If you're having trouble with the gift of prophecy in the church, you're probably having trouble with Scripture.

Let's look at the fourth chapter of Ephesians, beginning with verse 11. Notice the five special gifts listed. "He gave some, apostles; and some, prophets; and some, evangelists; and some, pastors and teachers." Most of us have seen real, live teachers and pastors and evangelists and even apostles, because *apostle* means "one sent," like missionaries. But most of us would deny ever having seen a real, live prophet.

Yet it is God's purpose that the gift of prophecy be in His

71

church. In Ephesians 4:12 we can read that the function of the gifts, including the gift of prophecy, is "for the perfecting of the saints, for the work of the ministry, for the edifying of the body of Christ: till we all come in the unity of the faith, and of the knowledge of the Son of God, unto a perfect man, unto the measure of the stature of the fulness of Christ." Have we reached that stature yet? We still need all the gifts!

Some look back on the days of the prophets and say, "The prophets were for the purpose of helping immature, naïve people grow up. Now that the church has come of age and matured, the gift of prophecy is no longer needed." Don't believe it! The gift of prophecy will be needed "till we all come in the unity of the faith, and of the knowledge of the Son of God, unto a perfect man, unto the measure of the stature of the fulness of Christ: that we henceforth be no more children, tossed to and fro, and carried about with every wind of doctrine."

Evidently it has been God's purpose that this gift be always present, so that His people can have the advantage of detailed counsel, relevant to the time and age in which they live. Sometimes it is difficult to see how all the details from the prophets of old apply to our time. Even in the messages to this church written in the last century, it is not always easy, and we enter into a great deal of dialogue and discussion over it sometimes.

According to Scripture, the gift of prophecy is for the church. Don't go looking for a true prophet of God outside the church. The gift is for believers. Read 1 Corinthians 12:28 and 14:22. In Paul's analogy we can see a close similarity between prophecy and eyes. Evidently they saw the same analogy back in the days of the Old Testament prophets, for in those days the prophet was called a "seer," or see-er. 1 Samuel 9:9. As a boy, I wondered what the word *seer* meant until someone helped me understand. It's taken from the idea of seeing. The prophet was eyes for God's people.

It would be natural, then, to expect prophets to have visions. God said in Numbers 12:6 that He would reveal Himself through His prophets in visions and dreams.

Let's look at an Old Testament example of the practical function of a prophet. Second Kings 6, beginning with verse 8: "Then the king of Syria warred against Israel, and took counsel with his servants, saying, In such and such a place shall be my camp." He made secret plans in his own headquarters about the way to carry on the assault. Verse 9: "And the man of God sent unto the king of Israel, saying, Beware that thou pass not such a place; for thither the Syrians are come down. And the king of Israel sent to the place which the man of God told him and warned him of, and saved himself there, not once nor twice. Therefore the heart of the king of Syria was sore troubled for this thing; and he called his servants, and said unto them, Will ye not shew me which of us is for the king of Israel?"

One of his servants knew the answer. He said, verse 12: "None, my lord, O king: but Elisha, the prophet that is in Israel, telleth the king of Israel the words that thou speakest in thy bedchamber." There's nothing private in the enemy's camp when a prophet is defending God's people!

From this story we can see that God used prophets to solve real needs and relevant issues. As the needs of His people changed from time to time and from age to age, God sent other prophets with messages relevant to the changing situations.

In 1 Corinthians 1:7 we are told that in the last days it will still be God's purpose that the church come behind in no gift. He doesn't want us to come behind in apostles or pastors or teachers or evangelists—or prophets.

Well, if the gift of prophecy is to be in the church, whether in Bible times or at the end of time, we know that the devil will have a counterfeit. This is one of his regular methods. Whenever there has been a great truth from God, he has come in with a falsehood. The greater the truth, the greater his counterfeit. If God has a day of worship, the devil will provide a counterfeit. If God has the gift of prophecy, the devil will invent false prophets. Jesus warned us about this in Matthew 24:24. There's no point in having the false without the true, so He advised us to test the prophets by their fruits. See Matthew 7:20. In 1 Thessalonians 5:20, Paul said, "Despise not prophesyings." When you hear about the gift of prophecy, whether you're driving through Salt Lake City or Boston, Massachusetts, or elsewhere, don't despise it. Check it out. 1 Thessalonians 5:21: "Prove all things; hold fast that which is good."

As you study about the gift of prophecy in Scripture, you discover three ways in which the gift is manifested. First, in the ability, through the illumination of the Holy Spirit, to speak God's word. Prophecy can be simply to speak for God. Sometimes we confine it to prediction and fulfillment, but let's broaden it for a moment. A prophet is anyone who speaks God's truth for a particular time. In that sense, we may have more of the manifestation of the gift of prophecy than we would ordinarily think.

A second manifestation of the gift of prophecy appears in actual dreams and visions and the ability to make accurate predictions. This manifestation is rare. Some nowadays claim the ability to make predictions, but their claims usually prove false.

The third manifestation of the gift is even more rare. It has to do with being more than a prophet. The first incident of God giving "more than a prophet" to His people is recorded in Numbers 12:6-8. Moses had been sent by God to lead out a people who were to be His in a special sense. Aaron and Miriam, his brother and sister, were Moses' associates, and they became dissatisfied with his leadership.

In verse 2 of the same chapter, they said, "Hath the Lord indeed spoken only by Moses? hath he not spoken also by us?"

The Lord saw their attitude and was greatly displeased. He came to the tabernacle and said, "Hear now my words: If there be a prophet among you, I the Lord will make myself known unto him in a vision, and will speak unto him in a dream. My servant Moses is not so, who is faithful in all mine house. With him will I speak mouth to mouth, even apparently, and not in dark speeches; and the similitude of the Lord shall he behold: wherefore then were ye not afraid to speak against my servant Moses?"

Here God indicated to Aaron and Miriam that Moses was not only a prophet but "more than a prophet." God had a relationship with him and a function for him that included more than the term *prophet* signifies.

The second instance of someone who was "more than a prophet" occurs in the history of the Christian church. In Luke 7:20-28 Jesus is speaking: "What went ye out for to see? A prophet? Yea, I say unto you, and much more than a prophet. This is he, of whom it is written, Behold, I send my messenger before thy face, which shall prepare thy way before thee."

Jesus was referring to John the Baptist. He agreed that John was a prophet, but insisted that he was more than that. He was God's "messenger," sent at the beginning of the Christian church, when God was once again setting apart a special people.

I am going to suggest that the third instance, one that is particularly interesting to Seventh-day Adventists, is a young woman in the last century who was told that she was the Lord's messenger. Let me quote from her book, *Selected Messages*, book 1, page 34: "If others call me by that name [prophetess], I have no controversy with them. But my work has covered so many lines that I cannot call myself other than a messenger, sent to bear a message from the Lord to His people, and to take up work in any line that He points out." Page 32: "Early in my youth I was asked several times, Are you a prophet? I have ever responded, I am the Lord's messenger. I know that many have called me a prophet, but I have made no claim to this title. My Saviour declared me to be His messenger. . . . Why have I not claimed to be a prophet?—Because in these days many who boldly claim that they are prophets are a reproach to the cause of Christ; and because my work includes much more than the word 'prophet' signifies."

I am referring to the life and writings of Ellen G. White. I believe in them.

I suppose we are all aware that if you are against something, you can build a case against it, no matter what it is. If I decided to be against motherhood, I could build a case against it. I've seen some pretty raunchy mothers. I have seen mothers play tick-tack-toe with safety pins on the bottom of their baby's feet. I have heard of mothers who beat their children brutally. I have read of mothers who abandoned their children. If I were selective, I could bring together stories that would build a strong case against motherhood. I could build a case against apple pie too. I could tell stories of people who almost died from eating green apples. I could depict all the horrors of that experience. And if someone had never eaten apple pie, I might be able to prejudice him against ever trying it. If you're already against something, you can build a case against it, even if it's motherhood or apple pie.

But I believe in the gift of prophecy and in the messenger who was "more than a prophet," because I have found in them the voice of God to my own soul.

It was through this gift that I was led into an understanding of Jesus Christ and His righteousness. When I came into great trouble and was about to give up the faith, casting about for some kind of anchor, it was the depiction of the glory and kindness and beauty of Jesus in the book *The Desire of Ages* that captivated my attention. I've been intrigued by the fact that this little woman's favorite topic was the love of God. It wasn't temperance or hygiene; it was the love of God. It wasn't beating people over the head with their sins; it was the love of God. Some young people have the wrong image of this little woman; they think she must have worn black clothes and had a long face and a glum, gloomy personality. Not so.

Have you ever had trouble believing too strongly in prayer at times, because of aching knees? Have you ever been turned off by someone who would pray on and on, when you were hungry and anxious to get home? One day I read in her writings: "Long, prosy talks and prayers are out of place anywhere, and especially in the social meeting. Those who are forward and ever ready to speak are allowed to crowd out the testimony of the timid and retiring. Those who are the most superficial generally have the most to say. Their prayers are long and mechanical. They weary the angels and the people who listen to them. Our prayers should be short and right to the point."—*Testimonies for the Church,* vol. 4, pp. 70, 71. When I read that, I said, "Ten points for Ellen White! She's on my side. She's my friend." Then I read that no public prayer session should be longer than ten minutes, and no public prayer by any one person should be longer than two minutes. And I had timed some at five! (Forgive me for that!)

I took a class at the seminary from Arthur White, her grandson. He told human interest stories about her. Ellen White liked to make rag rugs. She made so many that James White, her husband, got tired of it. One day he walked up the steps of their home in Battle Creek singing a song he had just made up, "In heaven above, where all is love, there'll be no rag rugs there."

Ellen smiled, but she didn't give up making rag rugs. One day, not long after, her secretary came with a new, bright red dress and asked Ellen White what she thought of it. Ellen said, "I can hardly wait for it to wear out so I can put it in my rag rugs."

She was human. She was real. She didn't live in a cloistered cell somewhere. She was in touch with people and feelings and real things. One of the devil's masterpieces has been to turn young people off by a wrong use of her writings by uninformed, nit-picking people. If you will read for yourself what she said about the love of Jesus, you'll find that she is your best friend.

Take, for example, the chapter in *The Desire of Ages* titled "The Invitation," all about Jesus' invitation, "Come unto me, all ye that labour and are heavy laden, and I will give you rest." Another chapter that brings comfort and hope and peace is " 'Let Not Your Heart Be Troubled.' " In other chapters you will find classic descriptions, beautiful language that reaches the heart, about Gethsemane and the cross. Don't think that the only things Ellen White wrote were rebukes and reproofs. Have you given her a chance by reading for yourself?

It is possible to tear her writings apart and find fault with them. You can do the same with the Bible, and people have been doing it for a long time. But I believe that the writers of the Bible and the writer of our spirit of prophecy volumes were inspired by God in the same way.

Whether you are speaking of the gift of prophecy as demonstrated in Ellen White or the gift of prophecy in Bible times, there seem to be two areas of work that God gives His prophets. The first is to call an apostate people back to God; the second is to work within the revived people of God, giving them comfort, guidance, and special information. Notice that the function of comfort and guidance and warning has been in proportion to the faithfulness or unfaithfulness of God's people. Lamentations 2:9 indicates this. Here the prophet laments the condition of God's people. Referring sadly to Jerusalem, he says, "Her gates are sunk into the ground; he hath destroyed and broken her bars: her king and her princes are among the Gentiles: the law is no more; her prophets also find no vision from the Lord."

When the law was trampled and obedience ceased, the prophets received no vision from the Lord. But when God's people were revived and reformed, they had the function of the prophets in terms of special guidance, direction, warning, and comfort. If you study through the history of prophets, you discover this very definite trend.

I'd like you to read something you may not have read lately, *Testimonies for the Church*, volume 5, pages 76, 77, written at the end of the last century. "But few are heartily devoted to God. There are only a few who, like the stars in a tempestuous night, shine here and there among the clouds." "The patience of God has an object, but you are defeating it. He is allowing a state of things to come that you would fain see counteracted by and by, but it will be too late. . . . Who knows whether God will not give you up to the deceptions you love? Who knows but that the preachers who are faithful, firm, and true may be the last who shall offer the gospel of peace to our unthankful churches? . . . I seldom weep, but now I find my eyes blinded with tears; they are falling upon my paper as I write. It may be that erelong all prophesyings among us will be at an end, and the voice which has stirred the people may no longer disturb their carnal slumbers." Does that say anything to you about what we were referring to?

Suppose we had a real, live, honest-to-goodness prophet among us today, what would that prophet be saying? We'd get messages about television instead of about hoopskirts, don't you suppose? But there would be a note of comfort too. Here is something she predicted in *The Story of Redemption*, page 402: "I was pointed down to the time when the third angel's message was closing. The power of God had rested upon His people; they had accomplished their work and were prepared for the trying hour before them. They had received the latter rain, or refreshing from the presence of the Lord, and *the living testimony had been revived*. The last great warning had sounded everywhere, and it had stirred up and enraged the inhabitants of the earth who would not receive the message." Emphasis supplied.

We can see in this prediction something akin to Joel 2:28 in which God says that in the last days, "I will pour out my spirit upon all flesh; and your sons and your daughters shall prophesy, your old men shall dream dreams, your young men shall see visions." This was fulfilled on the day of Pentecost, in the early rain, and will be repeated before Jesus comes. Don't brace your feet when you hear about a prophet in the Adventist Church. It's predicted in the Bible. If you don't accept the genuine gift of prophecy, you don't believe the Bible. Test it. Pray for it. Seek the revival and reformation that will bring with it the revival of the gift of prophecy.

Now I'd like to paraphrase the story that we looked at in 2 Kings. Perhaps it will help us to understand a little more of the modern-day purpose for the gift of prophecy.

"Then the devil warred against God's people, and took counsel with his imps, saying, Such and such a place shall be my camp. This is my strategy. And the spirit of prophecy sent unto the leader of God's people saying, Beware that thou pass not such a place, for thither the devils are come down. And the leader of the people sent to the place which the spirit of prophecy told him and warned him of, and saved himself there, not once, nor twice. Therefore the heart of the devil was sore troubled for this thing, and he called his imps and said unto them, Will ye not show me which is for the leader of God's people? And one of his imps said, None, O devil, but the spirit of prophecy that is leading God's people telleth the leaders of God's people the words which thou speakest in thy bedchamber.''

If it was the function of the gift of prophecy in Old Testament times to save God's people from enemy ambush, would it not be the same today? Some are ready to throw out this gift to the church, but I would like to remind you that one of the greatest evidences of God's love is the guidance and hope and comfort of the gift of prophecy that saves us from being carried about by every wind of doctrine and deception. If you believe the Bible and the Bible only, you will accept this gift from Him.

Choose Ye This Day

Several years ago I was called by a zealous worker, a layman in the church, to go to a particular home on a particular evening to meet some people with whom he had been "studying the Bible" for several weeks. His method of study was to turn on the recorder and plug in the projector, and when the presentation was finished, unplug the machinery and go home. I was supposed to show up on this particular night, as pastor of the church, and get a decision. I had never met the people before. Their closest contact with Seventh-day Adventists was with a tape recorder and a projector! I can still remember how hopelessly futile the situation was.

There's an old evangelistic phrase that you may have heard, "getting people across the line." It refers to getting people to make decisions on particular points of doctrine. I'd like to point out that if people are not already across the line when distinctive truths are presented, that is not the time to get them across the line then! The commitment to Christ Jesus must come first. Until a person has been born again and has begun a relationship with Christ, there's no point in urging for decision on any other point.

Now there are several traditional methods of encouraging people to make decisions. The altar call is a good example. Some traditional methods are synthetic and artificial. Decisions are never to be forced by synthetic means. (What does the word *synthetic* mean? A synthetic product is a man-made imitation of something natural. An example would be nylon replacing silk. Silk is made by silkworms. If you magnify a piece of silk, the more it is magnified the more beautiful it appears. But when you magnify the synthetic imitation, the more you magnify it the worse it looks.)

So synthetic methods for getting people to make decisions are methods that are not based upon God's Word, but are invented by mankind as methods or gimmicks for trying to do God's work. What would be a synthetic way to persuade people to make decisions? What about man-made eloquence working on people's emotions? What about "salesman" techniques to "sell" the gospel? When we were studying speech in college, one of the things we debated for a long time was, Which is more important: what you say, or how you say it? How would you vote on that? Our teacher held out that it's far more important how you say a thing than what you say.

It is important how the gospel is presented. God wants it to be put in the most attractive light. But we sometimes go beyond that and work by synthetic means on emotions, using psychological leverage and herd instincts.

The Bible gives some very simple formulas for decision-making. The first I'd like to suggest is in John 10:1-5: "Verily, verily, I say unto you, He that entereth not by the door into the sheepfold, but climbeth up some other way, the same is a thief and a robber. But he that entereth in by the door is the shepherd of the sheep. To him the porter openeth; and the sheep hear his voice: and he calleth his own sheep by name, and leadeth them out. And when he putteth forth his own sheep, he goeth before them, and the sheep follow him: for they know his voice. And a stranger will they not follow, but will flee from him: for they know not the voice of strangers."

How does a shepherd herd his sheep? Does he lead them or drive them? He leads them. A group toured the Middle East not long ago. Before they arrived, the guide told them to watch, that even today they could see the shepherd leading his sheep as in Bible times. As fate would have it, the first flock they saw was being driven with sticks and stones. They checked to find out what had gone wrong and discovered that a butcher was taking the sheep to slaughter. Quite a difference!

Jesus said in Matthew 16:24, "If any man will come after me—" Notice the key word again. "If any man will *come after* me, let him deny himself, and take up his cross, and *follow me*." What do we mean by *follow*? We follow someone we are trying to imitate, someone who is setting the proper example, someone we admire and trust. We yield to him; he is our guide. It's the opposite of being coaxed or pushed or coerced.

In Revelation 14:4 we see a group of people just before Jesus returns who have become so involved with the One who is both Shepherd and Lamb that they follow Him wherever He goes. They are redeemed from among mankind. They are led by God's Word and His Spirit, and they depend upon Jesus.

Luke 9:57-62 tells about several who had trouble following Jesus. Verse 59: One "said, Lord, suffer me first to go and bury my father," let me go and say good-bye to the people at home. "Jesus said unto him, Let the dead bury their dead." This sounds cold and harsh if we don't catch the meaning of the context, that Jesus does not want divided hearts—He wants people with total commitment. Again, the key is to follow Him. First Peter 2:21 tells what we should do in decision-making, "Hereunto were ye called: because Christ also suffered for us, leaving us an example, that ye should *follow* his steps." Italics supplied.

We are invited to follow Him, not to run ahead or lag behind. The difference will be revealed to each person by the Holy Spirit. It would be possible for someone to get up and coax for a decision on a certain issue. For some people in the audience, it would be right on target. For others, it would be premature; and for still others, it would be the opposite. Only the Holy Spirit knows the timetable for every soul.

I remember making appeals for decision based on only two or three things. We would come to a particular topic in our public meetings and would try to divide everyone into these two or three groups. We'd appeal for everyone in the first category, then appeal for everyone in the next category. After the meeting, some would come and say, ''I didn't know which category I fitted into.'' Others would be offended because we had split the audience, and they felt conspicuous because they were not a part of any group. There would often be strangers in our meetings who didn't understand the points that were being discussed, and they would be offended.

Have you ever heard, ''Now, just before we close the meeting—'' and 45 minutes later, ''Now, just before we close the meeting, is there one more—''? But where do you find this in the Bible? Someone told me that at Mt. Sinai, after the Israelites worshiped the golden calf, Moses made an altar call. Study the story in Exodus 32. It's not the same thing at all. The people who responded came forward and were sent in to kill those who didn't. That was no evangelistic meeting! If that's the closest thing to an altar call you can find in Scripture, you'd better keep looking!

No, when it comes to encouraging people to make decisions, we are not to use man-made methods. We are not to capitalize on people's emotions. The Holy Spirit will do enough of that on His own. The Bible is full of appeals for people to make decisions, but we don't want to use nonbiblical methods.

As you become acquainted with people on a one-to-one basis, you become aware of the steps people take in approaching a decision. A few words spoken to someone in private when he is under conviction to decide for God are often more effective than a whole sermon given to a crowd. People have differing needs; they approach decisions from different directions, at different speeds. It is impossible to pick out two or three points and expect to fit everybody into two or three groups.

The primary issue in all spiritual decisions is conversion and surrender to Jesus Christ. The Holy Spirit is the primary force, not human devisings. Is the Holy Spirit big enough and capable enough to pull for decision in the hearts of people? Is it possible that some of our man-made methods to help the Holy Spirit actually hinder Him?

When we use the biblical methods of encouraging people to decision, people are more likely to remain approachable. Have you ever been in a situation in which you found that, because of the synthetic means used, people were unapproachable afterward? This often happens with young people. They are turned off, turned cold, by a synthetic approach.

There is a big difference between converting people to a set of church doctrines and beliefs, and having people converted, by the Holy Spirit's power, to Christ. Sometimes we equate the two, thinking they are the same. But they are not. The teachings of the church find meaning only within the framework of conversion to, and relationship with Christ.

The Bible is very clear that we must make decisions, and we must not put them off. Second Corinthians 6:2: "Behold, now is the accepted time." When? *Now!* One of the greatest leaders in decision-making was Joshua, who said in Joshua 24:15, "Choose ye this day."

Notice the rest of his words, "Choose ye this day *whom*

ye will serve." He did not say, Choose ye this day *what* ye will do, but *whom* ye will serve. It was an invitation to choose whose servant you would become. There's quite a difference between the two.

We are to beware of procrastination. Here is where thousands have erred to their eternal loss. The invitation is, "Choose ye *this day*." Italics supplied. If the Holy Spirit has been speaking to you concerning some need for decision in your life, don't put it off. The longer you wait, the harder it will be to decide, and the easier to keep putting the decision off.

Did you ever climb up onto the garage roof when you were a kid and had someone take the ladder away? You knew what you had to do then, didn't you? I remember sitting on the garage roof as a kid after everyone else had jumped. I knew I was going to be the offscouring of the neighborhood if I didn't follow them. The longer I waited, the less likely it was that I would ever jump. I learned that the only thing for me to do was to stand up and jump immediately and get it over with! It sounds kind of dumb, now that we are grown up, but it's from real life!

This sort of thing is not always confined to kids. I was grown up (but I wasn't grown up!) in Colorado, near a little place called Crystal, visiting one of those Outward Bound schools designed for rich people's kids.

Parents would pay hundreds of dollars for their children to go there for a month and take part in a most rigorous mountain-training program. On this Outward Bound program was an obstacle course that the kids went through almost every day. Some of us visitors got the harebrained idea of going through it. It would scare you just to look at it. You had to go on ropes through tree tops, swinging from one rope to another, catch the last one and swing on to something else. After falling off a lower rope and landing on my face in mud, I finally came to the final problem of the course. We had climbed up boards nailed to tree trunks and were way up high. Now we were supposed to bail out from up there into a net far below.

I discovered that all the youthful nerve I had developed on the garage roof was gone. As I stood there, everything went black and purple and yellow and blue! I closed my eyes, then opened them. I couldn't go back, I'd already burned those bridges. The people below were watching. What could I do? The longer I waited, the worse it got. Finally I closed my eyes and just kind of let loose. It wasn't nearly as bad as I had expected. Actually, it was a lot easier—when I finally decided!

The devil likes to see people procrastinate and does everything he can to make the decision for Christ look impossible. His biggest trick is to get people to put off deciding until some later time.

The story is told that one day the devil called for a committee to discuss with his imps ways and means to get mankind to be lost. He asked for suggestions.

One imp jumped to his feet and said, "I have a plan. We can tell people there is no God."

The devil said, "Sit down! All anyone has to do is look around at the sky and trees and flowers, and he will know there is a God. That won't work."

After a pause, another imp stood and said, "Why don't we tell people that the Bible is not true, that it is only a myth, a collection of fairy tales?"

The devil said, "Sit down! If people read the Bible at all they will see that its prophecies are fulfilled and will know that the Bible is true. That won't work either."

A third imp suggested, "We could tell them that God will not forgive their sins. They will be so discouraged, they will give up and we'll have them."

"Sit down!" said the devil. "That can never work now that Christ has died on the cross. No one will believe it who knows anything at all about Christ's sacrifice for sinners.''

There was a long silence. At last another of the imps slowly arose and said, ''I have a plan that I think will work. We will tell people that there is a God. We will tell them that the Bible is true. We will tell them that Jesus has made provision to forgive their sins. But we will add two words: Time enough.''

The devil jumped to his feet in fiendish delight. ''That's the plan that will work!'' he cried. The imps began to applaud. And that is the plan the devil has been using successfully ever since.

Probably every one of you has some decision that you've been toying with, thinking about, something that is heavy on your mind every time you're on your knees. One of the earmarks of a conviction from the Holy Spirit is that it is lightest when you are farthest from God and heaviest when you are closest. It grows until you are finally convinced that God is trying to tell you something.

But perhaps you are still thinking about it, still wondering. One of these days you expect to make a decision, so why not now? I invite you to make a decision. I have no idea what the decision should be. I'm not the Holy Spirit; I'm not God. But whatever decision you know you need to make, I invite you to decide.

Someone may need to make the decision to begin a meaningful devotional life, to seek to know God day by day. That's one I wish everyone would decide on. There may be some who can't make that decision until the Holy Spirit brings them to that point, but there may be someone reading these lines who is at that point and needs to make that decision.

Someone may be struggling with a conviction of the need to share or witness. Perhaps it's been weeks, or months, or years, and you have finally realized that you need to decide deliberately to reach out and serve and witness. You may need to decide that.

Perhaps you may need to decide to have family worship. You may need to put a sledgehammer through your TV set. For some, that could be one of the best decisions you could make. Then gold-plate the sledgehammer and display it over the mantel!

Someone may need to decide to return to God the 10 percent He asks of His people in Malachi 3. Some may have only recently learned some point of truth that we have studied in these volumes, something new to you, such as the Sabbath or one of the other pillars of faith. Some may need to decide that the second coming of Jesus is the most important event in your future and that you want to be able, by God's grace, to look up with joy when you see Him coming.

Someone may be struggling with a conviction of something you need to make right, or pay back to make restitution. It has been heavy on your mind, and the Holy Spirit is saying to you, "Decide!" Don't put it off any longer.

Perhaps someone has been convicted by the Holy Spirit to follow Jesus' example in baptism by immersion, the Bible method for public acceptance of Christ.

As you see, when it comes to decisions, the possible decisions are numerous. Only you know what decision is right for you. I join Joshua in appealing to you to make that decision now. To put off making a decision is, in a sense, to make a decision. But it's a decision for the wrong side.

In conclusion, I'd like to remind you that every conviction concerning a particular *thing* is only a test concerning a particular *Person*. God leads His people along step by step, to different points calculated to test what is in the character. Some people do well at one point but fall off at another. What would be the purpose, for instance, if God were convicting me to put the sledgehammer through my TV? The TV itself might be only a secondary issue. The real issue would be my love for Jesus, my personal, daily relationship with Him, and my continuing devotion to Him.

Whatever decision is made concerning behavior has to do with surrender and trust in a Person. When Joshua said, "Choose ye this day *whom* ye will serve," he was simply reminding us of the fact that decisions are based on relationship with Christ, and the *things* are simply tests or evidences of that relationship.

For the one who has already made the commitment to fellowship and relationship and surrender to Jesus, the struggle over the surrender of things becomes far easier, because in a sense, those decisions have already been made.

The major decision always has to do with love for Jesus and relationship with Him. Have you settled that? Have I settled that? I invite you to settle it now and make your decision for Him.

Read All of the

Common Ground talks about the many beliefs we hold in common
with other faiths including the second coming, the divinity of Jesus,
and righteousness by faith.

In **Uncommon Ground** Morris Venden discusses the doctrinal pillars
of the Seventh-day Adventist faith, most of which are not shared by
the rest of the evangelical world.

Venden Trilogy

Higher Ground looks at several additional doctrines, all vital to the message the church must bring to the world in these closing hours of history.

These information packed books are available now at your local Adventist Book Center. Credit card holders may dial the toll-free 800 number to order their books.

Toll-free telephone order numbers for credit card purchases:
1-800-253-3000 in Continental U.S. except:
1-800-253-3002
in Alaska and Hawaii

1-800-843-8585
in Central California

1-616-471-3522
in Michigan (call collect)

1-800-435-0008
in New England

1-800-547-0612
in Northern California

1-800-522-2665
in Oklahoma

1-800-452-2452
in Oregon

1-800-263-3791
Eastern Canada ABC

Higher Ground
Foundations for Faith/3
Morris L. Venden

1984 Pacific Press Publishing Association

Other Dynamic Books by Morris Venden

What Jesus Said About. . .
Some of the most pressing problems of the Seventh-day Adventist Church today are addressed in this book.

Good News and Bad News About the Judgment
Some fresh thoughts about Pharisees, legalists, performance and the judgment.

The Pillars
Morris Venden defines the pillars of our faith and assures us that if we study their significance, we will be given increased light and understanding.

The Return of Elijah
You have already heard about the three angels, but did you know about the three Elijahs? A vivid application of what the Christian life is all about.

Available now at your local Adventist Book Center or call toll-free for credit card purchases.

Toll-free telephone order numbers for credit card purchases:

> 1-800-253-3000 in Continental U.S. except:
> 1-800-253-3002 in Alaska and Hawaii
> 1-800-843-8585 in Central California
> 1-616-471-3522 in Michigan (call collect)
> 1-800-435-0008 in New England
> 1-800-547-0612 in Northern California
> 1-800-522-2665 in Oklahoma
> 1-800-452-2452 in Oregon
> 1-800-263-3791 Eastern Canada ABC

© 1984 Pacific Press
Publishing Association

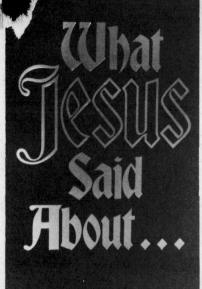

What Jesus Said About . . .

Morris L. Venden

Good News and Bad News

About the Judgment

Morris L. Venden

The Pillars

Morris L. Venden

The Return of Elijah

Morris L. Venden